THE MODERN ORGAN

BY

ERNEST M. SKINNER

WITH

ILLUSTRATIONS, DRAWINGS, SPECIFICATIONS

AND A

BIOGRAPHICAL SKETCH

OF

Ernest M. Skinner

BY

T. SCOTT BUHRMAN

THE ORGAN LITERATURE FOUNDATION
Braintree, Massachusetts 02184

This book is an unabridged republication of the original
and is available from

THE ORGAN LITERATURE FOUNDATION
Braintree, Mass. 02184

ISBN 0-913746-11-8

To

ARCHIBALD T. DAVISON, Ph.D.

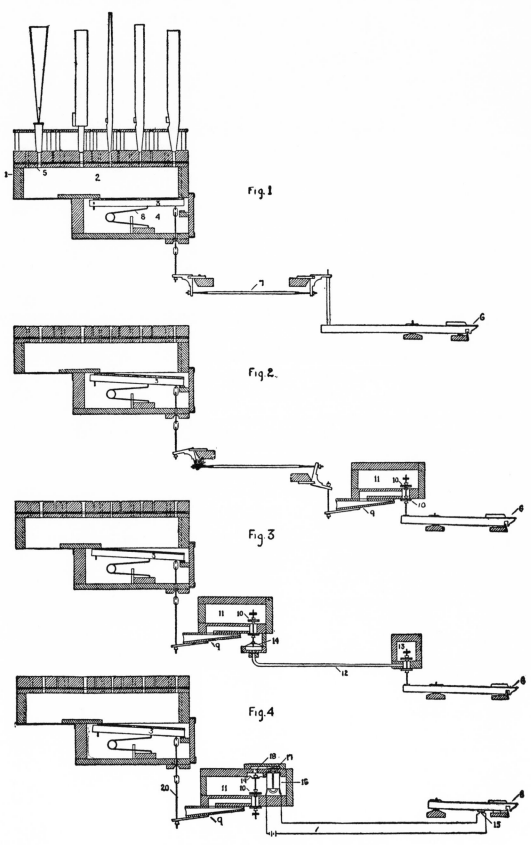

Fig.1

Fig.2.

Fig.3

Fig.4

ILLUSTRATING THE EVOLUTION OF THE KEY ACTION

The Modern Organ

CHAPTER I

EVOLUTION OF THE ACTION

It is the purpose of this work to describe the modern organ, with such reference to its predecessors as becomes necessary for purposes of comparison.

Organs may be divided into two classes: *i. e.*, those having mechanical actions and those having tubular or electro-pneumatic action. This division is made on account of the fact that the mechanical action prohibits the use of heavy wind, as the wind pressure is reflected in the key touch, and is therefore limited. In other words, this arbitrary classification is not made on account of the actions *per se*, but in view of the fact that the modern organ, with its magnificent power and wealth of orchestral color and perfection of mechanism, is made possible wholly through the disassociation of the touch and the wind pressure.

In the accompanying diagrammatic drawings, Figure 1. represents the principle of the tracker action.

No. 1 is a wind chest upon which stand the pipes of the various stops belonging to a manual.

No. 2 is a chamber common to all the pipes of the same note standing on the chest.

No. 3 is a valve within the air Chamber 4, the purpose of the valve being to admit air from Chamber 4 to Channel 2, and from thence to the pipes according as they are put in communication with said Channel 2 by means of the Slides 5.

No. 6 is a key which, when depressed at its outer extremity, transmits its motion to Valve 3 by means of its chain of action 7.

As the wind pressure in Chamber 4 tends to close Valve 3, it is obvious that when Key 6 is depressed it must overcome both the weight of the Spring 8 and the resistance of the air against Valve 3. It is also obvious that any increase in the wind pressure against Valve 3 will correspondingly increase the resistance of the key touch, which is, therefore, limited in this form of action to what can be comfortably overcome by the finger. We say "comfortably" advisedly, as, in very large instruments having this type of action, the resistance of the key, owing to the necessarily great size of Valve 3, has made such demands on the strength of the player as to be well-nigh prohibitive.

About the year 1833 Charles Spackman Barker, an Englishman, brought out a device which he called a "pneumatic lever." The principle of which is diagrammatically illustrated in Figure 2. It will be seen that the chain of mechanism shown in Figure 1 is interrupted in Figure 2, by the introduction of Pneumatic Motor 9.

Figure 2 operates as follows:

When Key 6 is depressed it raises a stem supporting Valves 10; said valves serving, first, to admit air pressure to Pneumatic Motor 9 from Pressure box 11, and second, to allow it to escape to the atmosphere when the key is released. The pressure serves to expand Motor 9 which then moves the chain of action leading to the valve, formerly operated by the finger. When the key is released, the Valve 10 within Pressure box 11 closes communication with the wind pressure and opens it to the atmosphere, allowing Motor 9 to deflate, permitting Valve 3 to close. It will be seen that the labor of the finger is now limited to the amount of pressure necessary to operate Valve 10 and that the much greater labor of operating Valve 3 is now performed by the Pneumatic Lever 9. It is also obvious that the size of Valve 3 is no longer limited, as the Motor 9 may be made sufficiently large to perform any labor required of it. The introduction of the pneumatic lever was a tremendous advance over the original mechanical action, but the chain of action from key to valve, while greatly increased in efficiency, was still cumbersome and slow in action, as viewed from present-day standards.

There appears to be some doubt as to who was the originator of the tubular-pneumatic action. Its general principle may be observed by a study of Figure 3.

Pneumatic Motor 9 has been removed from its proximity to the Key, as in Figure 2, and placed directly beneath Valve 3. The mechanical connection between Key and Valve is now practically eliminated, a column of air contained in Tube 12 now serving as a means of communication between them.

A primary valve-box, with valves identical in structure to the one shown in Figure 2, but of lesser dimensions, is now located above the keys, as shown in Figure 3. When Key 6 is depressed, air from Chamber 13 is admitted to Tube 12, through which a pneumatic impulse is imparted to Motor 14, thereby raising Valves 10, which were formerly raised by the Key, as in Figure 2, resulting in an operation of Motor 9, identical with that previously described with reference to Figure 2. The great weight of mechanism and consequent sluggishness incident to a mechanical construction has now given place to a column of air, resulting in an increase in the capacity for speedy operation, which, as far as the action is concerned, is only limited by the capacity of the performer. Further advances witness the disappearance of the tubes and key valves, in place of which appear, as in Figure 4, a contact at the key, a modified form of valve at Motor 9, operated by a magnet, the magnet in turn being energized by an electric circuit, opened and closed by the key contact, all of which combined represent the elements of the electro-pneumatic action.

The operation of this electro-pneumatic action is as follows:

When Key 6, Figure 4, is depressed, Contact 15 closes the circuit leading to Magnet 16, thereby energizing this magnet, drawing down armature Valve 17, closing the passage leading to air chamber 11 and opening to the Atmosphere Duct 18. Wind pressure in Chamber 11 by means of Diaphragm 19 then operates Valves 10, Motor 9, Valve 3, thro Link 20, as described in Figure 2. Figure 4 shows the electric action in its operative position.

In the evolution of electric action, much difficulty was experienced in the development of successful contacts and armatures. Armatures were made adjustable, which resulted in much maladjustment and irregularity. Contacts were made of various substances—gold, platinum, silver and phosphor bronze, with an idea of overcoming the oxidization incident to the sparking at the contacts. Experience has shown that the design of the contact is more important than the material of which it is made. Contacts having a slight rubbing motion, thereby cleaning themselves, prove to be entirely reliable—the most common and successful metal in use being phosphor bronze. Gold, platinum and silver are alike unreliable, if there is not a slight rubbing at the contact. When the slight rubbing exists, the phosphor bronze is equally serviceable and much less expensive. It is also necessary to have sufficient resistance in the magnet windings to reduce to a minimum the amount of current used. This also serves to decrease the sparking at the contacts.

In the best forms of fully developed actions, the armatures and contacts are very reliable, requiring no attention or adjustment, the armatures having a predetermined and unalterable movement.

The last and final great stumbling block to a perfect mechanism was the slide chest. A curious misunderstanding prevailed regarding this crude type of construction (which is the one shown in Figures 1, 2, 3 and 4), namely, that the large valves furnished a better attack than the smaller valves, as constructed in the modern type of wind chest which is so designed that each pipe has its own valve. This supposedly superior attack of the slide chest valve has been called "the pneumatic blow." The large size of the valve was supposed to admit an amount of air so greatly in excess of the demands upon it that a kind of blow or concussion resulted which was favorable to the speech of the pipes.

If a slide chest valve were opened very promptly, an organ pipe would undoubtedly speak more promptly than would be the case if it were opened slowly, but not for the reason supposed. The slide chest valve formed one side, or more strictly speaking, the bottom of an enclosure. When it was suddenly pulled in a direction away from the enclosure (Channel 2), it resulted in a partial vacuum within said Channel 2, this channel thereafter undergoing a transition from a condition of partial vacuum to one of atmospheric pressure, and from atmospheric pressure to organ pressure, the same being a gradual advance from the minus condition to the full bellows pressure which would show that, instead of receiving an impact of air, the pipes experienced a progressive or cumulative delivery of wind. That this is what the pipes require is fully indicated by the improvement in speech occasioned by the nicks placed in the lips of the pipes, by the voicer, in order to obtain a proper speech and to which a later reference will be made.

It was possible to open these large slide chest valves with promptness through the pneumatic agency, but, since they depended upon a spring for closing, it is obvious that they must close much more slowly; in fact, a pipe would be very slow indeed in speech, if it could not utter a tone before the valve closed, and this, as much as anything, gave rise to the impression that the slide chest valve afforded a more favorable condition for a perfect attack.

The individual valve of the modern chest is more speedy in its operation than the pipe itself. In the lower notes a valve may open and close in the one-hundredth part of a second, which is less time than an 8-foot pipe requires to develop its tone. The sluggishness of the slide chest valve gave large pipes more time for speech, but prohibited the speed in operation, for which the modern individual valve chest is so remarkable.

The modern chest affords perfect articulation, with speed and silence in the stop action.

Inasmuch as it is possible to open and close the valves of the lower notes in a modern wind chest more rapidly than the pipes will speak, it is obvious that an organist should understand the acoustic limitations of the lower registers and govern his touch accordingly.

CHAPTER II

WIND PRESSURE

HAVING now arrived at a condition in which a mechanical interference no longer stands between the performer and his ability to perform, we proceed with the elimination of other defects which caused the organ to be regarded as "inexpressive," "inflexible" and on a low artistic musical plane.

First among these defects was the variability of the wind pressure.

In instruments of twenty years ago and less, the usual method of construction was to make one large bellows, to load it with broken stone or bricks in order to establish a pressure and force the wind from the bellows, and then to operate the bellows with a water or electric motor, acting on reciprocating feeders. Wind trunks leading from the bellows delivered the wind to the several divisions of the organ at distances varying from five to twenty-five feet. An unvarying pressure, or anything approaching it, was an impossibility.

A later construction provided a main bellows as before, but introduced small compensating reservoirs at the point of demand, but, inasmuch as these reservoirs were also weighted, we still find an unsteady, though vastly improved, wind pressure.

Contemporaneously with the above construction, an increase in wind pressure found favor and this made it necessary to construct bellows of much greater strength.

Further increases in wind pressure outran the resources of the bellows maker and it soon became evident that other means would have to be found to meet the situation. Several installations were made in which a single rotary, centrifugal fan-blower of ordinary type was employed. These had to be run at a high speed and were noisy, subject to breakdown and difficult to manage. During this period, springs took the place of weights on the compensating reservoirs and with this improvement there appeared for the first time in the history of organ building a perfectly steady and unvarying wind pressure; so unvarying, in fact, that the tremolo, for a few years, almost went out of effective existence, as the wind could not be shaken.

The question of wind supply was finally solved by the multiple fan, which consisted of a number of fans mounted on a single motor-driven shaft, each fan occupying a compartment of its own, and all serving equally in the labor of raising the pressure to the point desired.

5

If the pressure to be developed was fifteen inches and there were five fans in the blower, they would be run at a speed necessary for any one of the fans to develop three inches. The fan nearest the inlet would accordingly develop three inches and deliver it to fan No. 2, which raised it three inches more and so on through to fan No. 5 which delivers it to the organ at the final pressure of fifteen inches. Inasmuch as the pressure is developed in multiples of three inches it is evident that the blower will deliver any intermediate pressure between three and fifteen inches, as for example a 9-inch pressure may be taken from the third fan, by means of an intermediate outlet at fan No. 3. As the multiple fan delivers its maximum capacity on instant demand, the large main reservoir becomes unnecessary for storage purposes and is accordingly discarded. The blowing equipment now consists of the multiple fan and the compensating reservoirs at the point of delivery to the pipes, and this is the final solution of the problem of wind pressures, unlimited as to quantity or pressure and of a steadiness above criticism.

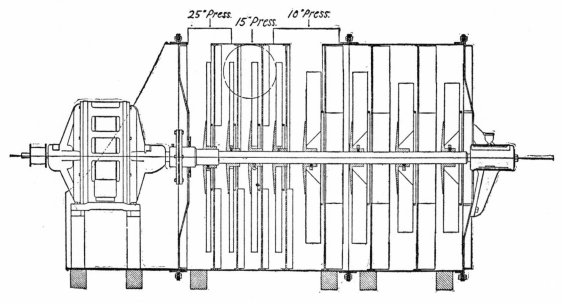

FIG. 5

It might be regarded as a paradox that an unshakable wind pressure may be shaken with a tremolo. As the tremolo is closely related to the question of steadiness of wind, it will be next in order for consideration.

A usual test for defective wind pressure is to draw full swell, with sub and super couplers, to hold a single note in the upper octave of the keyboard and to strike staccato chords in the lower register. If variability exists, it will be at once apparent in the unsteadiness of the treble note. If unsteadiness is not evident under this severe test, the tremolo will be found ineffective.

All first-class modern instruments will meet this test easily. Special provision must now be made to produce a tremolo. This may be done in one of two ways. A common way is to place a revolving fan above the pipes. This does not produce a true vibrato but results in a sort of yammer-yammer-yammer. A tremolo should be identical in quality with the vibrato of a well-trained voice, spontaneous and devoid of departure from a true wave-line. A true tremolo is never produced by mechanical means, but depends for its degree of perfection on other elements.

A period of inertia is the first requisite. This is obtained by placing a small weight on the reservoir supplying wind to the manual which the tremolo is to affect. This weight causes the reservoir to hold back slightly, whether the reservoir is rising or falling. While the weight affects the pressure only one-tenth as much as the springs on this same reservoir, the springs do not lag behind, as they are without inertia.

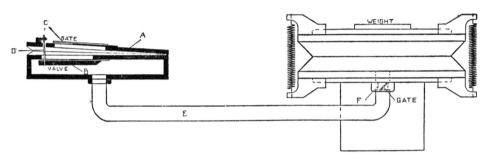

Fig. 6

Having applied the weight the tremolo will now be found to be effective, but we have lost something. Under our test for steadiness we find we have suffered a partial return to the condition we labored so many years to escape. What is the solution?

Investigation shows that the lower octave of any stop requires as much wind as the remaining four octaves together. It is obvious that if the lower octaves of all the larger winded stops be placed on separate chests fed by separate wind trunks, they will be isolated from the smaller pipes and cannot affect their wind supply or steadiness. Having done this, if we repeat our test, we now find the wind perfectly steady under the new conditions and we have an effective tremolo as well. The separate chests upon which the large pipes are placed are called "bass chests."

Having now made it possible to shake the wind, the next question is how to shake it.

Means for providing an intermittent escape of wind is the usual device and is entirely satisfactory, if carried out scientifically.

A shake may be produced by a simple valve arranged to open and close an outlet; the valve being mounted on a pivoted lever balanced by springs and counterbalanced by a weight, the whole being enclosed in a box.

This device is as crude as it is common. It is also inclined to be noisy and has little range of adjustment and its effect is ambiguous as to quality.

A most perfect tremolo is produced by a small hinged pneumatic, A, Fig. 6, to which air is admitted through its lower leaf by a supply valve, B, one inch wide and ten inches long. The upper leaf of the pneumatic has a slide C for regulating the escape of air. The upper leaf is made movable, and the lower stationary and forming the upper part of an enclosure containing the supply valve. This supply valve is hinged at one end and is connected to the movable leaf of the pneumatic by a threaded stem D at the other and rises and falls with it. Air is admitted to the enclosure containing the supply valve by means of a conductor F connecting the tremolo with the compensating reservoir in which the wind is to be shaken. The entire point of the situation lies in the length of the conductor E connecting the reservoir and the tremolo. If the conductor is too large or too short, the tremolo will be too rapid and noisy and not amenable to adjustment.

To produce an effective tremolo in a reservoir under a six-inch wind pressure will require a three-inch conductor fifteen feet in length. There should be a damper valve E at the reservoir end of the conductor to govern the amount of wind entering the conductor.

The speed is regulated at the slide on the movable leaf of the tremolo. The intensity of the tremolo is adjusted at the damper valve in the conductor. The tremolo itself, in a really spontaneous shake, is only a primary to set up an initial intermittent pulse.

When the tremolo register is drawn, the upper leaf of the tremolo engine falls, opening the supply valve beneath it. This allows air from the conductor to pass into the tremolo pneumatic in a larger quantity than can escape through the slide in the top of the tremolo, which therefore inflates, and in rising closes the supply valve and so falls again and is ready to repeat the process.

If all the conditions and processes are as they should be, the amount of air escaping at the outlet is very small. However, this is, as stated, only the initial event in the process.

As the air in the conductor next to the tremolo escapes, the air in the entire column starts after it. When the rising tremolo closes the supply valve, the column experiences a check and a rebound results; this rebound and succeeding escapements and rebounds, constitute a reciprocating recoil which requires a very slight functioning of the tremolo to perpetuate it. The dynamic force of this recoil is large in comparison with the initial impulse produced in the tremolo and, as stated before, its intensity depends on the amount of air involved, as determined by the damper valve.

If this recoil is once established, the quality of the tremolo is assured and the frequency is, relatively, of small importance.

It required much time and patience to establish these principles, but it was a labor worth while.

The use of bass chests for the large pipes not only makes it possible to produce tremolos of great musical value without interfering with the steadiness of wind, but has other points of excellence of far greater import.

The basses were formerly placed on the chest itself or, if this congested the pipes too much, they were located on blocks placed near the chests and the wind conveyed to them from the main chests by means of conductors. These conductors frequently conveyed the wind for considerable distances with a consequent loss of pressure through friction, which caused the tone of the pipe to suffer and become windy.

When the large pipes are placed on bass chests, they stand over valves of their own which are actuated by small tubes in communication with the main chests.

The bass chests are located at the ends and in the rear of a swell chest, for example, so that the large pipes stand against the wall of the swell-box and may be supported by it. This position gives them ample room for speech and is much better construction than any other arrangement. It should be borne in mind that where the large pipes stand on, or are supplied with wind from the main chest by conductoring, it is impossible to make the wind steady. The bass chests should have a wind supply *independent* of the main chests.

Having isolated the large pipes, it now becomes possible to lay out a chest scale in such a way that all the remaining pipes have ample room for speech. The conditions as regards the placing of the pipes are now so much improved over the original construction that unreliability in speech, windiness, or faulty articulation is almost inexcusable.

CHAPTER III

THE SWELL-BOX

THE swell-box, a most important detail of the organ, is not generally understood to this day.

The effectiveness of a swell-box depends on three conditions, of which the first is the contents of the box.

An equipment of stops of little power and cumulative value will never produce an effective crescendo. In order to get something big out of a swell-box there must be something big within it, to come out.

The second condition is that a swell-box shall have the proper dimensions. Boxes having great depth in proportion to their width are not effective. Even though the shutters are wide open, the tone will be smothered.

A swell-box should be wide or high, and shallow from front to back, not more than half as deep as it is wide.

The third condition is a well-fitted shade.

In planning specifications for an effective organ, the swell-organ should be provided with a full equipment of chorus reeds of 16-foot, 8-foot, and 4-foot pitch, a good Diapason 4-foot Octave and mixture. These six stops on a good pressure and well voiced will insure a fine crescendo, providing the rule for the proportions of the swell-box and tight shutters is observed. Whatever is done to make the swell-box effective with regard to the chorus work, will be equally favorable for the softer stops.

The operation of the swell-shades by electro-pneumatic agency was a stubborn problem. This device usually took the form of opposed pneumatic bellows, connected to each other and to the swell-shades. One of these pneumatics was supposed to open and the other to close the shutters. The valves which controlled the pneumatics had to be sufficiently large to cause them to move the shades from the open to the shut position with expedition. These same valves were also expected to supply the pneumatic for moving shorter distances. When the machine was moved slowly from one extreme position to the other, the transition took the form of a series of hysterical jerks; a pneumatic frequently went too far and was kicked back again by its *vis-à-vis*, as this arrangement made each half of the device exceedingly jealous of the other. An oscillation called "hunting" was a common occurrence,

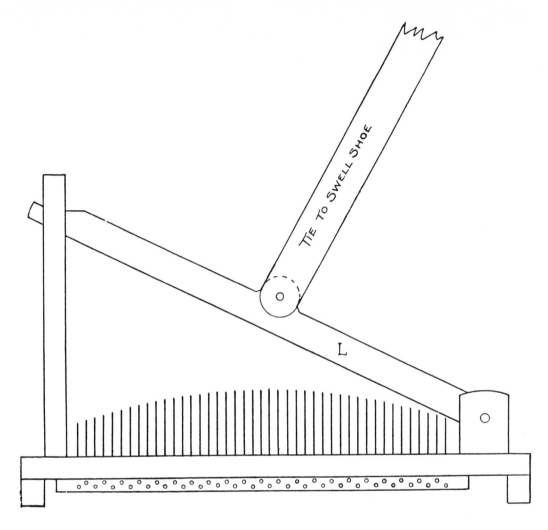

FIG. 7

"In this crescendo pedal the battery is permanently connected to the movable lever L and each of the wires placed beneath it is in circuit with a magnet controlling a stop of pipes. As the lever moves downward, the electric current flows from the lever to the terminal wires in regular succession, the terminal wire nearest the pivotal point of the lever receiving the current first, the others following."

in which event the organist moved the swell-shoe to another position and hoped for the best.

The defect in this machine was in that it furnished a uniform power for a widely varying load.

The perfected swell engine is a marvel of efficiency. It will move the swell-shades their entire traveling distance, or one-sixteenth the distance, in the same amount of time. It puts the swell-shades under the control of the organist in a way unapproached by the mechanical action, which is more than was ever hoped for. It relieves him of a physical labor which prohibited a real flexibility, and leaves little between his thought and its expression.

All of which is due to a provision in the design of the motor, *i.e.*, its power varies with its load.

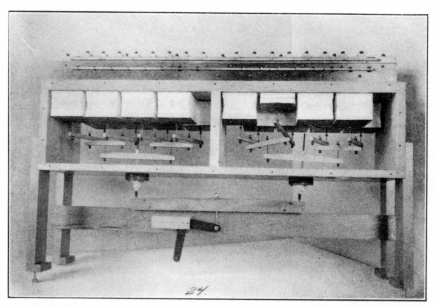

FIG. 8

In the electro-pneumatic swell engine shown in Fig. 8, there are sixteen pneumatic motors. Each motor, (through a system of floating whiffle-tree levers,) moves the swell-shades one-sixteenth their total motion. If the swell-shoe is moved suddenly from one extreme to the other, all the motors work at once but the labor of each motor is always the same. As *all* the motors will move as quickly as any one of them some remarkably effective Sforzando effects may be obtained. The motors close the shades and a spring opens them. Each motor is operated by its own magnet.

In the days of the tracker pneumatic action there appeared a device for drawing the stops successively in order to produce a crescendo. This was very complicated and required power pneumatics as large as a compensating reservoir which were arranged to bring on the stops through the action of

FIG. 9

Organ in the Minoriten-Kirche in Bonne at which Beethoven presided.

Beethoven, at the age of 11, learned to play on this organ and played daily from the old note-book seen in the picture.

FIG. 10

Console of the Organ in the Cathedral of St. John the Divine, New York City.

drums, cams, rollers and trackers.   It required about fifteen seconds to build up to the full organ and as much more to back out again.   It weighed several hundred pounds.

The mechanism of a modern crescendo, Fig. 7, suitable for an organ of 100 stops, weighs about six ounces.   It is operated directly by a pedal.   Its speed in either direction depends on the inclination of the operator.

The Console of a high grade modern organ is a very handsome affair. The interior finish is in polished mahogany.   The draw stops are of solid ivory of a size to permit of clear and distinct lettering.   They are placed at an angle of 43 degrees, facing the player.

The Keys have the "tracker touch," i.e., four-oz. initial and one and one-half oz. when depressed.   This makes the organ and piano touches almost identical, so that practice on either instrument is of equal value and not an interference, as was the spring organ touch to the piano, before the "tracker" touch became an accomplished fact.

Stops are controlled collectively by combination pistons, which, as they are made "adjustable," move the stops promptly and silently in any pre-determined way.   As the combinations visibly affect the stops, they may at all times be operated by hand, either to increase or reduce an active combination.

There has been considerable controversy as to the merits of the visibly operated combinations versus the invisible or dead combinations.

Every organist of note prefers the visible combinations.   The lesser lights are persuaded that the invisible are the more desirable—by their builders.

Consoles of the past and present may be compared by examining cuts 9 and 10.

CHAPTER IV

THE "AUGMENTED" PEDAL

THE "augmented" pedal is supposed by many, including a few organ builders, to be a makeshift or form of swindle intended to defraud the unwary. It is for this reason that the following explanation is given.

The idea of the augmented pedal is not new. It originated in England and the idea is at least thirty years old, probably more.

It consists in a construction that permits of drawing the pedal stops at either sixteen- or eight-foot pitch.

There is a fundamental reason why this is good practice with regard to the pedal organ and radically wrong when applied to the manuals. The manuals are played in chords, the pedal idiom is one note at a time. In the common chord of "C" on the manuals, if a four-foot stop be taken from an eight-foot stop, there will be, if both stops are drawn, one "C" less sounding than if both stops were complete in themselves. In the event of larger chords, doublings and omissions are more pronounced. This is of course the case with all manual octave couplers.

With the pedal organ the conditions are wholly different as chords are seldom played on the pedals. It is therefore clear that the effect of an eight-foot stop is not discounted by any probable use of its sixteen-foot relative. In the construction of the augmented pedal, all the stops to be augmented are carried one octave higher in order that the scale of the stops of eight-foot pitch may be complete.

Broadly speaking, if fifteen stops be drawn on a pedal organ of the so-called "legitimate" type, and a key depressed, there will be fifteen pipes sounding. If the same fifteen stops of the augmented pedal be drawn, there will also be fifteen pipes sounding.

The construction of the augmented pedal eliminates useless material.

The greatest difficulty in the proper laying out of an instrument is usually a lack of sufficient room. The use of the augmented pedal idea is the one thing that makes an adequate pedal possible in such cases. The term "adequate" implies both variety and power. The diagrams will clearly illustrate the way in which space is conserved and variety obtained. Figure 11 is a diagram of an augmented pedal.

A 16-foot Diapason and 16-foot Bourdon are diagrammatically shown.

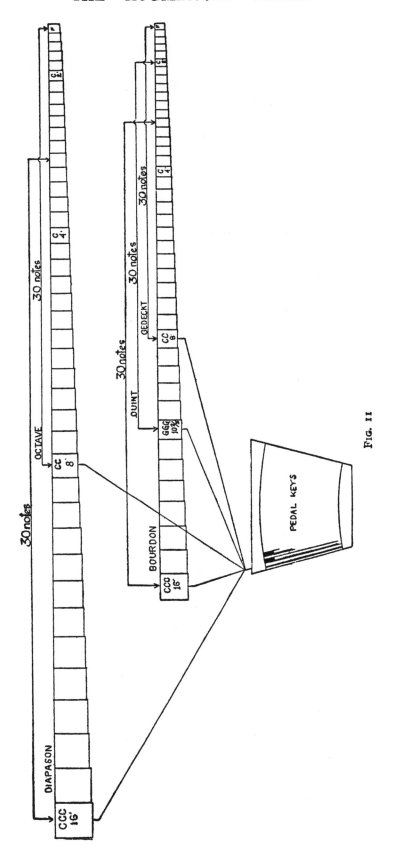

FIG. 11

From the 16-foot Diapason an 8-foot Octave is taken and from the 16-foot Bourdon an 8-foot Gedeckt and 10⅔ Quint are derived. If these five stops be drawn and a pedal key depressed, the 16-foot and 8-foot C's of the Diapason group, and the 16-foot and 8-foot C's and the 16-foot G of the Bourdon group are sounded as indicated by the lines connecting the pedal key with the five pipes named.

Figure 12 is a diagram of the "legitimate" pedal of exactly the same capacity as shown in Figure 11.

We now draw the five stops and get a response from five pipes as before, but we must not fail to note the fact that the 8-foot C of the Diapason, the 8-foot C and 10⅔ G of the 16-foot Bourdon now stand idle while other pipes exactly like them are doing the work they formerly did. This is presuming there is plenty of room and money to incorporate all this extra material.

In point of fact, there is seldom either room or money to provide for a "legitimate" (?) pedal of any such scope and completeness as the augmented pedal easily provides.

If, for example, prejudice excludes the augmenting principle, using our Figure 11 for illustration, we simply cancel the 8-foot Octave, 8-foot Gedeckt and 10⅔ Quint from our specification, as there is insufficient room for more than these two ranks in five cases out of ten.

Again, a stop that is obtained by augmenting costs less than one-half the amount necessary to pay for a complete additional stop.

On account of the cost, lack of space, etc., one will rarely find more than one stop of the 8-foot Flute family in the unaugmented pedal. This will be found to be too loud for soft effects and too soft for loud effects, a nondescript of no particular use, but costing, unfortunately, more than both the 8-foot Octave for loud effects and the 8-foot Gedeckt for soft effects in the augmented pedal. It is also more than likely that it is crowding its neighbors, more or less to their disadvantage.

Pipes of large scale require ample breathing space. The augmented pedal affords an ideal solution of this question of space and makes possible in almost every instance, a pedal of power and variety.

The only fraud that may be perpetrated with the augmented pedal is to deny the purchaser the advantage of the very substantial saving resulting from this type of construction.

We may go further than this, and say, in the knowledge of what the augmented pedal means to an instrument, that even if no saving were to result from its use, it is decidedly to be preferred on account of its musical advantages. The augmented pedal is the most effective musically from every point of view.

A most satisfactory detail of the system of augmenting is found in its application to the Swell 16-foot Bourdon, called in the pedal group, Second

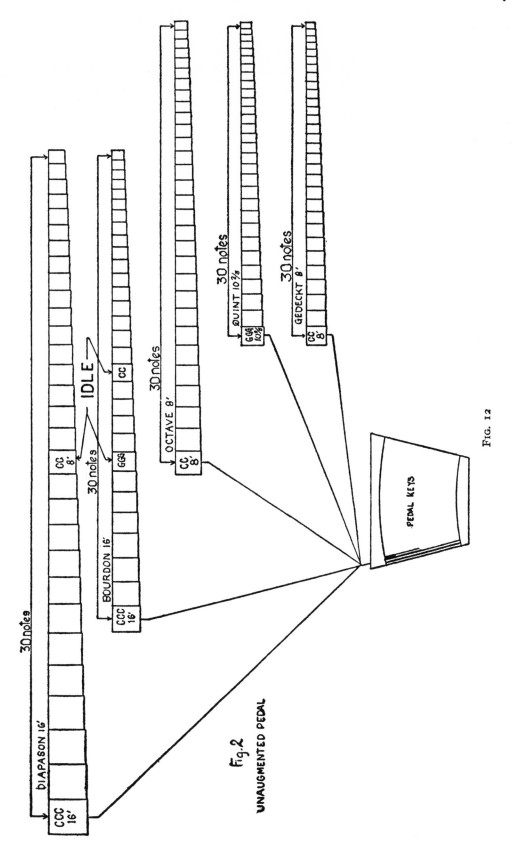

DIAPASON 16'

30 notes

CCC
16'

CC
8'

IDLE

BOURDON 16'

30 notes

CCC
16'

GGG

CC

30 notes

OCTAVE 8'

CC
8'

30 notes

QUINT 10⅔'

GGG
10⅔

30 notes

GEDECKT 8'

CC
8'

PEDAL KEYS

Fig. 2
UNAUGMENTED PEDAL

FIG. 12

Bourdon or sometimes Echo Lieblich.   In practice the lower 44 notes of this stop are made interchangeable with the Pedal.   This enables it to be drawn at both 16-foot and 8-foot pitch on the Pedal, leaving the Swell manual entirely clear for any suitable soft effect, as an 8-foot Unda Maris.   The Second Bourdon by itself is somewhat lacking in definition in its lower register; its 8-foot relative, the Still Gedeckt, lends a most beautiful and indispensable point and clearness in combination with the 16-foot Second Bourdon.

Some idea of the economy referred to may be gained from the fact that the 8-foot Still Gedeckt is figured at $50.

Criticism has been made that since no pipes have been added on account of the Second Bourdon and Still Gedeckt they contribute nothing to the full organ.   This is quite true.   The same would be equally true if suitable pipes had been added.   No pipes of suitable strength for the purpose will ever count in the forte.   The same may be said of the Æoline.   It is inevitable that loud voices overshadow soft ones.

The Swell Bourdon, used as a pedal stop, has the further advantage of being inclosed in the swell-box.   Its strength may be tempered to its associated soft stops.   This applies both to its 16-foot and 8-foot pitches.

If a 16-foot and 8-foot stop be drawn and an octave held there will be one 8-foot tone missing from the group of three pitches sounding, but the missing note is the same in pitch and quality as one already held and its loss is therefore so slight that it could hardly be detected by a trained ear.   This is the one point that may be taken as favoring the position of those against the augmented pedal.   Against this we must weigh a lack of both power and variety. A deficiency in power *and* expressiveness or variety is the glaring fault of the organs of the past.   A swell 16-foot reed that can be drawn independently on the pedal is a most beautiful bass for certain types of strings and it is also subject to the swell-shades.   Granting room and money for one 8-foot independent pedal stop, that cannot in any way whatsoever equal three 8-foot stops, loud, medium, and soft, which may be obtained by augmenting, without crowding, at a less cost and one of them in a swell-box.

Even if money and space were unlimited, it is obvious that augmenting would still enhance the musical value of a pedal organ.

It is a curious scheme that insists that it is a damage to use a pedal stop in simple octaves in a toe and heel technique when it is regarded as perfectly legitimate to use octave couplers in a chord formation on the manuals where the position is at least five times as objectionable, assuming that the pedal keys were played in octaves all the time, and where if the pedals are not played in octaves no objection holds valid.

The Pedal organs in the Cathedral of St. John the Divine, College of the City of New York, St. Thomas' Church, Grace Church, Fifth Avenue Presbyterian Church, Fourth Presbyterian Church and others of like caliber are all built on the augmented principle.

CHAPTER V

DISCOVERIES IN ACOUSTICS

HAVING followed the development of the mechanical side of the organ from its crude condition of twenty years ago to its present perfection of refinement, a consideration of acoustical discoveries is next in order.

The movement of the air in and around a speaking pipe is a very simple performance. Perhaps its very simplicity accounts for the fact that it has remained an unsolved problem up to the time the writer undertook a series of experiments, the result of which is here published for the first time.

In order that the vague uncertainty surrounding the phenomena may be fully realized, and a comparison made with the present account of the speech of organ pipes, quotations are given, the first of which is taken from *Tyndal on Sound*, lecture 5, page 183:

"You will have no difficulty in understanding the construction of this open organ-pipe, Fig. 95, one side of which has been removed so that you may see its inner parts. Through the tube *t*, (foot of pipe) the air passes from the wind chest into the chamber C, which is closed at the top, save a narrow slit e d, through which the compressed air of the chamber issues. This thin air current breaks against the sharp edge (upper lip of pipe) a b, and there produces a fluttering noise, the proper pulse of which is converted by the resonance of the pipe into a musical sound." Turning to page 184 we find: "This it also does, when for the pulses of tuning forks we substitute that assemblage of pulses created by the current of air when it strikes against the sharp upper edge of the *embouchure*."

In a treatise on the *Construction, Repairing and Tuning of the Organ*, published in Boston in 1905, page 52, we find: "How a Pipe Vibrates." "After the wind has been admitted into the foot of the pipe, it rushes through the windway in a thin sheet, which is directed against the upper lip. The mouth or space between the upper and lower lip now being covered with this current of air, the stream of air covering the mouth is exposed on the outside to the pressure of the atmosphere, while on the inside it is protected from it by the body of the pipe."

"The atmospheric air that passes out through the mouth of the pipe is forced upward, and against the burnished part of the pipe, which results in an inward draught beneath, and through the mouth. This inward moving draught on the outside of the mouth being stronger than the air at rest within the pipe, the sheet of wind passing through the windway gives way for an instant, and the inward bearing draught breaks through and passes into the pipe, which is immediately overcome by the power of the sheet of wind. This in its turn is most powerful until the draught overpowers it again, which produces a periodical movement of the air against the upper lip of the pipe. This periodical movement of the air takes place with greater or less rapidity, corresponding to the proportions of the mouth, and the pressure of the wind, which sets in motion the air in the body of the pipe. The elastic action of the lower end of the column of air in that portion of the mouth, aids, by compression and expansion, in restoring in turns the sheet of wind and inward bearing draught." This seems somewhat involved.

In Audsley's *Art of Organ Building*, Volume I, Chapter IX, second paragraph, we read: "The sound of a labial organ pipe is generated at its mouth by the rapid vibratory action of the wind stream which rushes from its windway setting up shocks, pulses, or tremors throughout the internal column of air. This much we know to be the case but beyond this simple and evident fact we acknowledge we know very little." Quoting from Mr. Hermann Smith, Mr. Audsley says on page 368, same volume, fourth paragraph, "From the time of Savart it has been known that the nodal division of the open organ pipe does not take place at the exact half of the length, that the half nearest the *embouchure* is the shorter of these 'unequal halves'— a contradictory term apologized for yet sanctioned, I believe, by the late Professor Donkin."

Again on page 369, third paragraph, we read: "Science brings forward no better plea than the surmise of a probable place, somewhere exterior to the mouth, which the air wave of the *lower half* of the pipe has to attain before it can be properly said to be completed in length." Truly an illogical conclusion if this line of reasoning is carried out.

On page 372, first paragraph, we read: "Again, why—seeing that both the lower and upper parts of the air column in an open pipe are in a state of tremor—is no sound produced anywhere but at the mouth of the pipe." On page 372, third paragraph: "Scientific investigators have made several attempts to reconcile the lengths of the vibrating air columns within pipes with the theoretical wave-lengths generated in unconfined air."

With reference to the speech of reed pipes, Mr. Audsley says on page 398, "It must be borne in mind, so as to understand the mechanical action of the tongue, that it at no time absolutely closes the openings in the reed. If it bedded perfectly on the surface of the reed it would be incapable of springing away from that surface in the manner it does." Next paragraph, "How the action of the tongue produces sound can only be guessed at and probably will never be known with absolute certainty." Again on page 399, first paragraph: "We suspect that here the air wave going up and down in the body is the cause but cannot picture to ourselves the nature of the proceeding, as the laws which have become known to us through the behavior of labial pipes do not hold good here." When the body of a labial pipe is reduced in scale to obtain the proper pitch it must be increased in length; in a lingual pipe the reverse is the case.

It will be seen from the above quotations that several questions are raised and some statements made; *i. e.:*

What happens when a flue pipe is speaking;

What happens when a reed pipe is speaking;

The variability of the node is unaccounted for;

The tone of a pipe all comes from the mouth. (Some hold with equal positiveness that it comes from the top.)

Attempts have been made to reconcile wave lengths within pipes to wave lengths in unconfined air without success;

The speech of reed pipes will never be understood;

A reed tongue never wholly closes its opening;

Reed and flue pipes are governed by dissimilar laws.

It is the purpose of this chapter to remove all the points of uncertainty enumerated and to show the almost universal error of the premises set forth.

The Tyndal theory depends on the air issuing from the flue and striking the sharp edge of the upper lip and dividing itself thereon. Inasmuch as this flame of air, which is technically known as the wind-sheet, does not touch the upper lip at all, this theory falls to the ground.

The second theory also assumes this error, in addition to which it states another condition which does not exist, namely:—that the wind-sheet is protected from the atmospheric air on one side by the body of the pipe. In fact, if such were the case, the result would be exactly opposite to that described.

We shall have to look for another explanation, as both the foregoing are founded on a condition which does not exist.

In the following explanation, let A, Fig. 13, represent the point where wind enters the foot of a pipe, and B the "flue" where it escapes. C represents a column of air enclosed by the body of the pipe. When wind escapes at the mouth of the pipe, it takes a direction as represented by line D, Figure 14. Its forcible exit causes an impact or blow to be given to the air just outside the point of issue, and its immediate vicinity. This attack of the wind-sheet on the air around the mouth of the pipe tends to drive it away from the point of issue. Part of it is driven toward the open air and accomplishes nothing, the balance is driven into the interior of the pipe. Having entered the body of the pipe at the base of the air column C it must, in order to progress farther, drive the whole of said column ahead of it. Having weight and a consequent inertia (the same being a disinclination to move when still, and a further disinclination to become still when in motion) the air column C declines to move on such short notice; in fact it balks.

However, the attack of the wind-sheet is not without result. The column of air has refused to get out of the way, but it has had to compromise. On account of its elasticity, it has increased its density, or become compressed at its base, and we will indicate this as in Figure 14, by the sign +.

The compromise, however, is only temporary, as the condition represented

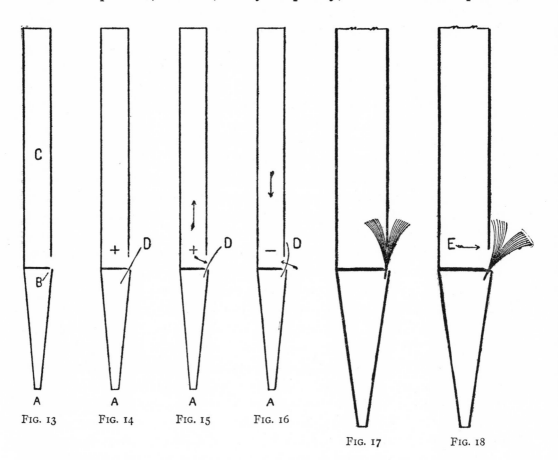

FIG. 13   FIG. 14   FIG. 15   FIG. 16

FIG. 17   FIG. 18

by the plus sign seeks to eliminate itself as naturally as water seeks its level. This it does by expansion. The result is twofold, *i.e.*, the column of air C is moved upward, and the wind-sheet D is bent out as at Fig. 15, the direction of the thrust of the air pulses being indicated by the arrows.

The column of air having moved upward for a certain distance, atmospheric pressure is now reached within the pipe. But the weight of the air carries it by the point of rest to such an extent that instead of the + sign we formerly had, we now have a − sign indicating a partial vacuum,

Fig. 16, in degree about as much below the atmospheric pressure as the + sign was above.

Therefore, obedient to the partial vacuum, the air just expelled from the pipe rushes back in again, both at the top and at the mouth, and again the momentum of the air carries it by the condition of atmospheric pressure we are seeking. In re-entering the pipe, the air pulses at both the top and mouth, must always operate in exact opposition to each other, as they are servant to a common influence, namely,—the condition indicated by the − sign. As a pulse of air has now issued from our pipe, and returned again, we have produced a sound wave. We have done more, we have established a condition which makes it necessary to go over the same ground again, for when the pulse of air rushes down the pipe, the pulse rushing in at the mouth dragged the wind-sheet over toward the pipe as at Fig. 16, causing it to meet the downward pulse, and establish that + sign again as firmly as ever, and that is what will continue to happen as long as the wind-sheet is present.

To recapitulate and condense we may restate the process as follows:— A stream of air attacking an enclosed column of air at one end compresses it at point of attack. The compressed content in expanding causes a pulse or sound wave to move upward through enclosed column, and outward at the mouth thrusting back the attacking wind-sheet. The momentum of said pulses causes them to over-run, resulting in a partial vacuum where compression formerly stood. Obedient to influence of vacuum, pulses re-enter enclosure, and over-running, again restore compression at center of activity, and receive an added impulse from returning air stream, completing cycle, and repeating it until air stream is discontinued.

The cycle at center of activity may also be expressed thus $+O-O+O-O+O-O+$, the O indicating atmospheric pressure.

The erroneous idea of the behavior of the wind-sheet is usually illustrated as at Fig. 17. The true condition is represented at Fig. 18. This is easily proved by attaching a movable vane to the front of a pipe as shown in Fig. 19, when the pipe is speaking the vane will be supported in a fixed position as is also shown in Fig. 19, if a bit of cotton wadding be dropped into the top of the pipe while it is speaking it will fall to the bottom and very likely issue from the mouth. These two tests taken together tell a convincing story.

In all metal organ pipes and in small wood pipes, the division between the foot and body is "nicked" at the point passed by the wind-sheet. Through these nicks small amounts of air escape, somewhat nearer the mouth of the pipe than the main wind-sheet. These serve to attack the air column more gently than would the main wind-sheet, setting up a preliminary sound wave, which however, as it gains in strength, finally seizes the entire wind-sheet, bending it back and forth, obedient to its will. It is a fundamental principle of good voicing that the wind-sheet must be absolutely dominated by the sound wave within the pipe.

If there is any condition about the mouth of a pipe that gives a character to the wind-sheet that makes it difficult to bend, it will result in a poor tone. To illustrate:—if too much air enters the foot of a pipe, the wind-sheet will be proportionately rigid, and consequently more difficult to bend. In such circumstances, we say the tone is hard or forced. Again, if the "nicking" is insufficiently deep, we lack the preliminary attack, and the budding sound wave finds it difficult to manage the wind-sheet. This results in a lack of firmness in the tone and a breathy asthmatic quality, and uncertainty of intonation.

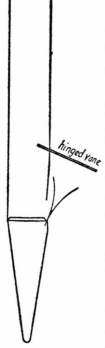

The cycle of the changing sign is present in all flue and reed pipes, although in a reed pipe a vibrating tongue takes the place of the wind-sheet and performs an identical office.

A narrow high mouth is characteristic of the modern organ pipe. This construction is essential in the use of high pressures, and for the following reason. The wind-sheet where it issues from the flue is very rigid, having a high pressure behind it. It would be impossible to bend it at this point. The wind-sheet expands in proportion to its distance from the point of escape, its density becoming less as it expands. The sound wave seizes the wind-sheet at the level of the upper lip, as at E, Fig. 18, and easily oscillates it, at this more flexible point. There is as much air to manage as before but it is more tractable.

There are different opinions as to where the tone issues from a pipe. Some hold that it comes from the top, and others with equal positiveness assert that it issues from the mouth. It should be clear from the account here given that it emanates from both the mouth and the top, and this is a

FIG. 19

true statement of the case.

We may go further than this and say that in a properly built pipe the tone emanates in some degree from the body of the pipe. The material from which either a wood or metal pipe is built should be neither too light nor too heavy, but should be made suitable to the wind pressure upon which it is to be voiced. A material that is too light on a ten-inch pressure may be exactly adapted to a five-inch wind. On the other hand, a pipe suitably heavy for a ten-inch pressure will be "tubby" on a five-inch pressure. There is no set rule for the weight of any pipe except that the thickness and weight of its walls should be adapted to its tone and pressure and that a correct thickness will permit of a slight vibration of the walls of a pipe, in sympathy with its tone, yet sufficiently rigid to maintain its integrity and not heavy enough to be wholly unresponsive to its influence.

In the older type of pipes, the mouths were very wide and much less in height. They were not adapted to high pressures because the width of the mouth allowed the escape of more air than the sound wave could control. This difficulty could be only partially corrected by cutting the mouths higher. Shutting off wind at the toe improves the tone but fails to utilize the high pressure which leaves us with a high-pressure outfit and a low-pressure result. The above is given to illustrate the impracticability of rebuilding old organs, or of using old pipes in new organs, and accomplishing a result that will equal, or in any way approach the quality of new pipes in a new instrument. *Such a plan is a mistaken economy, unless the pipes are reconstructed.*

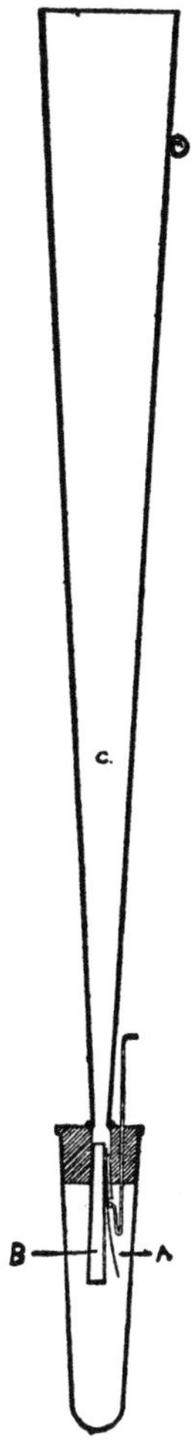

Two pipes of *equal length* but of different diameter will not sound notes of the same pitch. If a small pipe is to be made to sound the same note of the scale as a large one, it must be made longer. The pitch of a pipe may also be made to vary by blowing it more forcibly. Audsley has devoted much space in his voluminous work to this unaccountable behavior on the part of these "intractable agents." He quotes from several writers on the subject, one of whom refers to it as "the variability of the node." Mr. Audsley shows drawings of three wood pipes of widely differing scale and length, all sounding the same note, for which he and the authorities quoted, find no satisfactory explanation. Mr. Audsley is led to reject the sound wave theory entirely. It remains only to state that this problem is one of the foolish things that confound the wise. It presents a solution so obvious that it is childish. To solve:—

A Diapason pipe 24 inches long sounds a middle C.

A Salicional pipe to sound the same note must be 24½ inches long.

A complete sound wave must traverse the full length of a pipe and return. The sound wave in the Diapason must, therefore, be 48 inches in length, and that in the Salicional 49 inches.

Fig. 20

Both pipes are sounding a note of the same pitch, which leaves us but one conclusion:—the sound wave of the Salicional, perforce moves faster than the wave in the Diapason, as it moves 49 inches while the Diapason is moving 48. Hence the speed of a sound wave varies with the scale of the pipe, and also with a variation in wind pressure.

The speed of a sound wave is affected in several ways, *i. e.*, by temperature, wind pressure, scale and shape of pipes. Undoubtedly there are as many different speeds of sound waves as there are pipes in an organ.

We may now seek a reason for the variation in pitch of organs caused by changes in temperature.

It is well known that the more forcibly a pipe is blown, the sharper its pitch becomes. A change in temperature does not affect the wind pressure, which remains constant. Consequently a sheet of wind issuing from the mouth of a pipe always has the same degree of intensity. As the temperature rises, a pipe contains less air than before as some has left it through expansion. The remainder is lighter than formerly. It is, therefore, more forcibly excited by the wind-sheet, as the latter has not changed. The pipe is in effect blown harder. As the air becomes cooler, the process is reversed, and the pitch flattens.

We have seen in the flue pipe how an oscillating wave is set up within it and maintained by its reciprocal action on the wind-sheet. A study of the behavior of a reed pipe will show that its law, instead of being dissimilar to that of a flue pipe, is identical with it. When compressed air is admitted to the foot of a reed pipe, Figure 20, it rushes into the opening under the tongue and enters the lower extremity of the conical barrel or resonator. The rush of air into the opening under the tongue carries the latter with it and acting under this influence the tongue in a properly voiced reed closes its opening. The effect of the rush of air into the barrel is to cause the air in the pipe to move toward its open end in the form of a pulse, as in a flue pipe, and as in the flue pipe, its momentum causes it to over-run and produce a partial vacuum within the pipe, since air may no longer enter the resonator. The pressure within the foot of the pipe and the partial vacuum in the resonator now act in concert to close the tongue against the reed. A failure of the tongue to close at this critical point will defeat the action of the vacuum by an amount proportional to the leakage and gives the tone a windy inferior quality, so we may assume a tight closing of the tongue against its opening.

The momentum of the pulse of air carries it forward until it balances the action of the vacuum to hold it back, after which it immediately obeys the demand of the vacuum to come back into the pipe again. Owing to the conical shape of a reed pipe, a pulse of air going in either direction varies its speed in proportion to the taper of the pipe, so that the returning pulse of air reaches its maximum velocity within the reed just back of the tongue. Apart from losses caused by friction, the pressure of this pulse of air within the reed should equal the bellows pressure as it is a reaction caused by the action of the bellows pressure. So now we have pressures on both sides of the tongue about *equal to each other*. The spring or "curve" of the tongue now moves it away from the reed almost without opposition.

While the air pulse now is neutral to the bellows pressure, it is not neutral to the atmosphere, and as the momentum no longer exists and it is open to the atmosphere by way of the top of the pipe, it seeks repose by moving upward. This upward movement is assisted by and synchronous with another rush of compressed air into the reed which again moves the tongue to close its opening. The process is now complete and repeats itself as long as pressure remains in the foot of the pipe.

Inasmuch as a tongue has as natural a period of vibration as a resonator, it is obvious that for the production of pure tone, reed, tongue, and resonator should be made of a size most naturally in sympathy with the tone they are intended to produce, and that in regulating a stop of reeds great care should be used to get resonator and tongue in sympathy with each other, as otherwise they are liable to "fly off." If a reed is tuned "too sharp" it has a tendency to break into an interval a sharp fifth above as the resonator is then too flat in pitch for the tongue. This is a case identical in principle with that obtaining with regard to reeds in cold buildings. The temperature has not materially affected the tongues but it has, by increasing the density and consequently the amount of air within the pipes, made them proportionally flatter, giving them the same tendency to fly off that is noticed when they are tuned too sharp on the tongues.

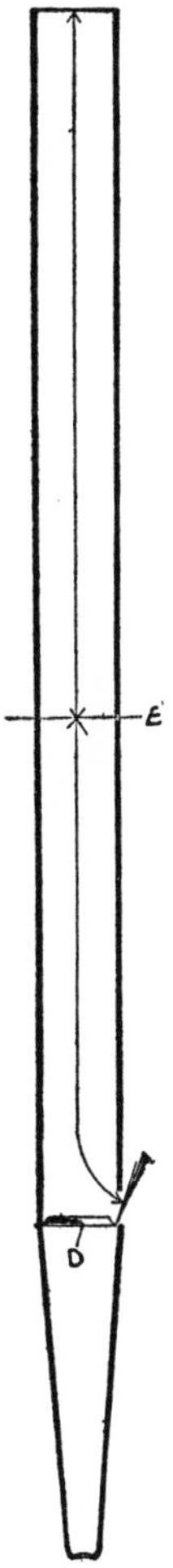

With regard to an increased length being necessary in a reed pipe with an increase in the scale, it should be borne in mind that reed pipes are tapered and flue pipes are not save in exceptional cases, and where they are tapered their lengths must be increased with an increase in scale exactly the same as in a reed pipe. Tuners know that the pitch of either a flue or reed pipe is made sharper by "coning it out" at the top, or flatter by "coning it in." The distinction between a reed and flue pipe with regard to the effect of tapering them is wholly fictitious and there is no principle in it other than is involved in expanding a pipe at its upper end to make it sharper. By making a pipe conical in shape the expanding is distributed throughout the scale instead of being confined to the upper end as in tuning. An increase in the diameter of any pipe, reed, or flue, at its upper end or throughout its length opens it to the atmosphere and shortens its acoustical length.

FIG. 21

That the nodal point in any pipe is below its physical center is well known. It is equally well known that shading the open end of a pipe tends to flatten its pitch. Yet the fact that the languid or partition between the foot and body of a pipe very largely obstructs its lower end has been completely ignored. A cylinder open at both ends would have a nodal point exactly in the center but why should it still remain in the center when a partition at one end has flattened the pitch a semitone? The languid acts to lengthen the pipe at its lower end and the nodal point moves downward to the acoustic center of the pipe which with very good reason is not coincident with the center of its length in inches. If the upper end of a pipe were shaded by a flat object to an amount equaling the shading by the languid, the nodal point would rise nearly to the center.

The effect of the languid, however, does not wholly account for the position of the node.

What Mr. Audsley terms the "Illogical conclusion" of Science surmise, of a "probable" place somewhere exterior to the mouth, which the air wave of the lower half of the pipe has to attain before it can be properly said to be completed in length, however illogical it may be, is in point of fact exactly the truth of the matter.

Referring to Fig. 21 and bearing in mind the behavior of the sound waves as demonstrated in Figs. 14, 15, 16, and 18, it will be clear that the downward movement of the sound wave must terminate at the wind-sheet, and this together with the flattening effect of the languid, exactly accounts for the position of the node below the center of the pipe. The effect of the languid includes making it necessary for the sound wave to turn a corner which has a retarding effect on its speed.

The great error of all time is in the presumption that a sound wave goes sailing serenely on through a conveyance of any size or description around corners and traveling at the *same velocity* regardless of the force propelling it, of its degree of confinement or of any other consideration whatever, in spite of the fact that there is plenty of obvious evidence to the contrary.

Lengths of pipes, besides being dependent upon scale also vary according to the wind pressure upon which they are voiced. These variations are taken care of by the ordinary means provided for tuning.

It is now clear that reed and flue pipes are obedient to the same law; why the nodal point is out of center; that the wind-sheet does not strike the upper lip, that the downward movement of the sound wave terminates outside the pipe; that sound issues from both the top and mouth of a pipe; that it is now possible to reconcile variation of wave lengths in and outside organ pipes; that a reed tongue completely closes its opening; that the behavior of a speaking reed is now clearly understood and need not be "guessed at" and that a careful reading of this chapter will show all these happenings to be very simple processes easily understood by anybody who does not take for granted an impenetrable fog of mystery and complexity.

CHAPTER VI

SPECIFICATIONS

THE advent of high wind pressures developed many improvements in tone production. Voicers were enabled to obtain promptness in speech, combined with power, in string toned stops, great sonority and purity in the Diapasons; Reeds of splendid brilliancy, solidity, and power, and a general improvement in tone, following the arrival of a perfected mechanical equipment.

Unfortunately the use of the new resources has not always been marked with good taste. A craze for the limit of characteristic possibilities left its mark on the production of the period. Excessively slender scales came into use. A serious sacrifice in quality resulted in the strings family, through this cause; an extreme acidity, coldness, and lack of blending properties.

This was but the natural outcome of suddenly acquired proficiency, a competitive test of skill, as it were. Experience, however, has done much to remove the tendency to over-emphasize, and a more conservative attitude is reflected in present methods.

A comparison of the two specifications to be found at the end of this chapter will bear testimony of the progress in orchestral imitation. In Example A, the French Horn and Orchestral Oboe are as near their prototypes as two horn players to each other. The English Horn has the covered, mournful quality of the orchestral instrument. The Clarinet is a true type, woody and rich. The Fagotto lacks little in imitative quality.

Of all orchestral qualities, the tone of the Violin has been least approached. The tone of a good Violin is warm, sympathetic, and has much "body" or fullness, and is rich in harmonies. Organ strings when used in two ranks of similar quality and tuned slightly apart, as in the Voix Celeste, probably suggest, in general effect, the nearest approach to orchestral strings possible. A Violin produces a vibrato only equalled by the human voice. The organ string is least effective in this respect. The organ string is, apart from its out-of-tune wave, only to be modified *per se* by the swell-box. The orchestral strings change in intensity, quality, and attack, and are seldom level; a sympathetic vibration is continually uttered by the body of the instrument which is wholly lacking in the organ string. Their only similarity is a richness in harmonies. The utter inability of the organ string to follow the orchestral in its kaleidoscopic variety forbids approach to a real parallel. So much for the imitative quality of the organ strings. As to their actual position in the general scheme of the instrument, they stand in equal importance with the other families of tone. While they do not closely resemble the orchestral variety, they are very rich in themselves; they combine remarkably with most other stops, and lend a richness and sparkle that no other family of tone affords. They may be varied widely in quality, from the ethereal shimmer of a Dulcet, to the broad sonority of a Gamba Celeste, which rivals three or four combined Diapasons in power.

The growth of modern high pressure reeds has been adequately accompanied by the development of Diapasons and wood flutes. Sixteen-foot chorus reeds on the manuals, however, have not always been suitably supported. The predominating note of the pedal organ is normally one octave lower than the pitch of the manuals. A sixteen-foot reed on the pedal, of whatever power, is not an adequate bass for a sixteen-foot manual reed, and there are, on most large organs, two or more of this character. A thirty-two-foot Diapason or Bourdon lacks both sonority and definition when used against 16-foot manual chorus trumpets. The thirty-two-foot pedal reed of large scale, and smoothly voiced, restores the balance. For this we have the Bombarde, which stands alone in its dignity and power.

Distinguishing the modern organ from its predecessor, we find an increased variety in the 8-foot work, a smaller proportion of mutation stops, the addition of orchestral color, and greater power and variety in the pedal division. To this we must add a perfect mechanical equipment.

The two specifications here given are of the organs in St. Thomas' Church, New York City, and St. George's Hall, Liverpool, England. A study of these specifications will disclose the difference in ideals of their respective periods of construction. The names of the stops are arranged in parallel columns for greater convenience in making a comparison.

ST. GEORGE'S HALL ORGAN   ST. THOMAS' ORGAN

GREAT ORGAN—25 Stops   GREAT ORGAN—17 Stops

16	Diapason	16 Diapason
		16 Bourdon
8	Diapason No. 1	8 Diapason No. 1
8	Diapason No. 2	8 Diapason No. 2
8	Diapason No. 3	8 Diapason No. 3
8	Diapason wood	8 Philomela
8	Stopped Diapason	8 Wald Flute
8	Violoncello	
		8 Erzähler
		8 Flauto Dolce
5⅓	Quinte	
4	Viola	
4	Flute	4 Flute

(*St. George's Hall Organ*)		(*St. Thomas' Organ*)	
4	Principal No. 1	4	Octave
4	Principal No. 2		
3⅕	Tenth		
2⅔	Twelfth	2⅔	Twelfth
2	Fifteenth	2	Fifteenth
2	Piccolo		
	Doublette		
	Sesquialtra		
	Mixture		Mixture
16	Trombone	16	Ophecleide
8	Trombone	8	Tuba
8	Ophicleide		
8	Trumpet		
4	Clarion No. 1	4	Clarion
4	Clarion No. 2		

SWELL ORGAN—25 Stops.		SWELL ORGAN—23 Stops.	
16	Diapason	16	Bourdon
		16	Dulciana
8	Diapason No. 1	8	Diapason No. 1
8	Diapason No. 2	8	Diapason No. 2
		8	Clarabella
8	Stopped Diapason	8	Gedeckt
8	Viol da Gamba	8	Gamba
8	Voix Céleste	8	Voix Celestes
		8	Salicional
8	Dulciana	8	Æoline
		8	Unda Maris
		8	Quintadena
4	Principal	4	Octave
4	Octave Viola		
4	Flute	4	Flute
2⅔	Twelfth		
2	Fifteenth No. 1	2	Flautino
2	Fifteenth No. 2		
2	Piccolo		
	Doublette 2 rks		Mixture 3 rks.
	Fourniture 5 R		Dolce Cornet
16	Trombone	16	Contra Posaune
16	Contra Hautboy		
8	Ophicleide	8	Cornopean
8	Trumpet	8	French Trumpet
		8	Oboe
		8	Vox Humana
4	Clarion No. 1	4	Clarion
4	Clarion No. 2		
8	Oboe		
8	Clarinet		
8	Horn		

CHOIR ORGAN—18 Stops.		CHOIR ORGAN—12 Stops.	
16	Diapason	16	Gamba
8	Diapason	8	Geigen Principal
8	Clarabella	8	Concert Flute
8	Stopped Diapason		
8	Dulciana		

(St. George's Hall Organ)	(St. Thomas' Organ)
8 Viol da Gamba	8 Dulcet 2 R
8 Vox Angelica	
	8 Kleine Erzähler
4 Principal	
4 Flute	4 Flute
4 Gamba	
2⅔ Twelfth	
2 Fifteenth	
2 Flageolet	
Sesquialtra	
	16 Fagotto
8 Trumpet	8 Flügel Horn
8 Cremona	8 Clarinet
8 Orchestral Oboe	8 Orchestral Oboe
	8 English Horn
	Celesta
4 Clarion	

SOLO ORGAN—15 Stops.	SOLO & ECHO ORGAN—20 Stops.
8 Diapason wood	8 Philomela
8 Viol da Gamba	8 Gamba
	8 Gamba Celeste
8 Stopped Diapason	8 Harmonic Flute
4 Flute	4 Flute
2 Piccolo	
16 Contra Fagotto	16 Contra Fagotto*
8 Bassoon	8 English Horn*
8 Trombone	
8 Orchestral Oboe	8 Orchestral Oboe*
8 Corno di Bassetto	8 Clarinet*
8 Trumpet	8 Flügel Horn*
8 Ophicleide	8 Tuba Mirabilis
8 Vox Humana	8 Vox Humana
4 Clarion No. 1	8 French Horn
4 Clarion No. 2	8 Diapason
	8 Night Horn
	8 Flute Celeste
	8 Vox Angelica ⎫ At other
	8 Æoline ⎬ end of
	4 Flute ⎭ Building
	8 Vox Humana

PEDAL ORGAN—17 Stops.	PEDAL ORGAN—18 Stops.
32 Diapason	32 Diapason
32 Diapason (metal)	32 Violone
16 Diapason (wood)	16 Diapason No. 1
	16 Diapason No. 2
16 Diapason (metal)	16 Violone
16 Salicional	16 Gamba
	16 Dulciana
16 Bourdon	16 Bourdon
	16 Echo Lieblich
8 Bass Flute	8 Octave
8 Principal	8 Gedeckt
	8 Still Gedeckt

*Interchangeable with Choir.

(*St. George's Hall Organ*)   (*St. Thomas' Organ*)

5⅓	Quinte..	
4	Fifteenth.....................................	
	....	8 'Cello
	Fourniture....................................	
	Mixture.......................................	
32	Posaune.......................................	32 Bombarde
16	Ophecleide....................................	16 Ophecleide
16	Contra Fagotto................................	16 Contra Posaune
8	Trumpet.......................................	8 Tuba
4	Clarion.......................................	4 Clarion

The St. George's Hall organ has one hundred stops and the St. Thomas organ ninety, of which five of the Solo are interchangeable with the Choir. Stops of similar character have been placed opposite to each other in order to show the two instruments in their true relationship.

Numerically the St. George instrument is superior by ten stops. This difference is almost entirely accounted for by mutation work. A comparison of the two schemes will be found most interesting and truly representative of the changing ideals of this epoch. It will perhaps also show something of the difference in national tastes.

CHAPTER VII

LOCATION OF THE ORGAN

AN organ may be perfectly made and voiced and yet be a failure in consequence of the unfavorable conditions of its surroundings.

The architect is as a rule glad to co-operate with the organ builder by providing adequate space and convenience, but there is little printed information of value on this subject and it is the purpose of this chapter to

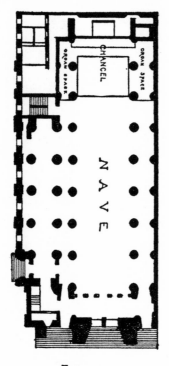

FIG. 22

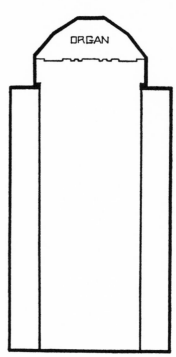

FIG. 23

outline some general rules which, if followed, will insure a satisfactory result as far as the conditions of a building are concerned.

The ceiling of an organ chamber should be made continuous with the wall or ceiling of the auditorium. Sound is reinforced, augmented, or reflected by flat surfaces and has a tendency to follow them. Voices travel far over still water but a slight ripple destroys its carrying property. A sound

FIG. 24

Fig. 25

produced in an organ chamber easily emerges and moves throughout a building if the walls of the chamber have been properly surfaced and the tone is unobstructed by arches or walls which tend to reflect it back into the organ chamber.

An example of an ideal location for an organ will be found in Figs. 22 and 23, in which the instrument stands in the auditorium, entirely open. Fig. 24 shows a photograph of an installation of this description, which is located in Finney Chapel, Oberlin, Ohio.

While as in Figures 22 and 23 the organ is outside the chancel proper, the space it occupies is, on account of its great height and slight depth, essentially an open one. Examples of this position will be found in the Cathedral of St. John the Divine, St. Thomas' Church, New York City, and in the Skinner Memorial Chapel, Holyoke, Mass. The shape of these areas provides that the instrument may be so put together that no portion of it obstructs any other.

A variation of this condition is to stand an equivalent organ space on end, as in the Fourth Presbyterian Church, Chicago, where great height but a comparatively small area was available. The organ was here assembled in what may be termed a perpendicular formation; the Swell over the Choir and Solo and much of the Pedal over the Great. The ceiling of the auditorium was sufficiently higher than the organ chamber to prevent difficulty with questions of temperature, usually caused by the divisions of the organ being at varying levels. Wherever possible the manual divisions of an organ should be on the same level.

In the above example, the lower notes of the pedal Violone are utilized as show pipes. See Fig. 25. In the central group of pipes in Fig. 24, the pedal 32' Violone also appears.

The statements made in a previous chapter in regard to the swell-box are equally true of the organ chamber, namely, a chamber should be twice as wide as it is deep and as high as it is wide. It is not true, as is commonly supposed, that an organ is better for having an unlimited space above it. While any general rule regarding proportions may be varied more or less, the rule is a safe guide and something definite to work to. A rule to break is better than no rule at all.

An organ chamber should never be open to a transept. When an organ is divided and placed on opposite sides of a building, the tone from each division should issue toward the other, otherwise people sitting in a side gallery or transept will hear one side of the instrument out of balance with the other, and in most cases the result is beyond a poor musical effect; it is oppressive and frequently makes these sittings so undesirable as to become useless.

Figure 26 illustrates an actual example of this description. Owing to the way in which the organ was laid out most of the tone passes into the transept. The swell-boxes face the transept opening and so direct the tone toward it and the transept gallery is rendered practically useless from a musical stand-point.

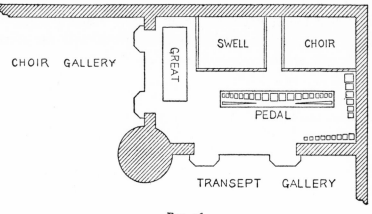

Fig. 26

Fig. 27 shows how this same organ chamber might have been successfully arranged. The swell-boxes face the choir gallery, the large pedal pipes have been placed more favorably, all the tone is magnified by hard surfaced walls and directed toward the choir, and the sittings in the transept gallery are as good as any in the building.

The exception to this rule will be found in buildings with very wide, high transepts where the organ is in a considerably elevated position. An example of this description will be found in St. Paul's Church, Toronto, Canada, where the organ chambers are also wholly open at the top.

The side openings do not enhance the result; they simply do not interfere with it. This is the only instance of the kind known to the writer. Where a side opening is very much higher than the floor of an organ chamber

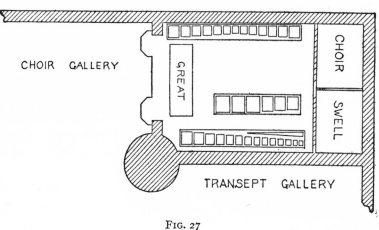

Fig. 27

so that the tone is directed toward the ceiling, the condition is not so unfavorable.

Beyond any question whatever the best result musically is obtained when the tone of the organ, wherever placed, is directed toward the singers. This prevents the disjointed, ill-balanced effect always present where tone designed to contribute to a common result, proceeds from several localities.

In Fig. 28 will be found a variation of Fig. 29, which fairly illustrates the position of the organ in the Cathedral of St. John the Divine, New York City. In Fig. 29, the tone is directed into the chancel, and becomes one with the voices of the choir. In Fig. 28, the tone issues towards the tran-

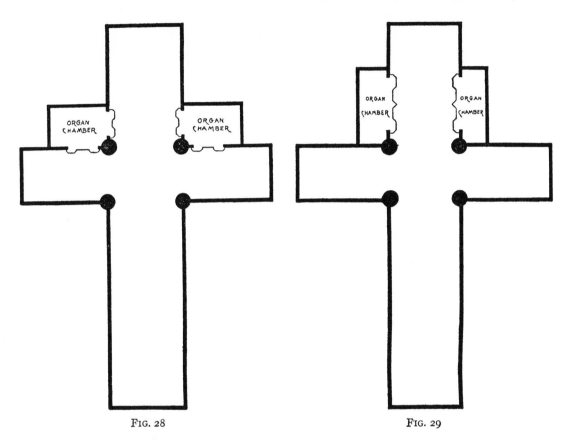

FIG. 28   FIG. 29

septs. A listener in either transept will hear the division of the organ nearest to him out of proportion to the other and to the choir, and both will hear the organ more easily than the choir. The smaller the building the more unfavorable the condition becomes.

Where the organ chamber in an existing building is poorly proportioned, a good result may be obtained by covering the walls with hard

FIG. 30

plaster, Keen's cement or King's Windsor cement, which gives a smooth surface and the greatest possible resonance.

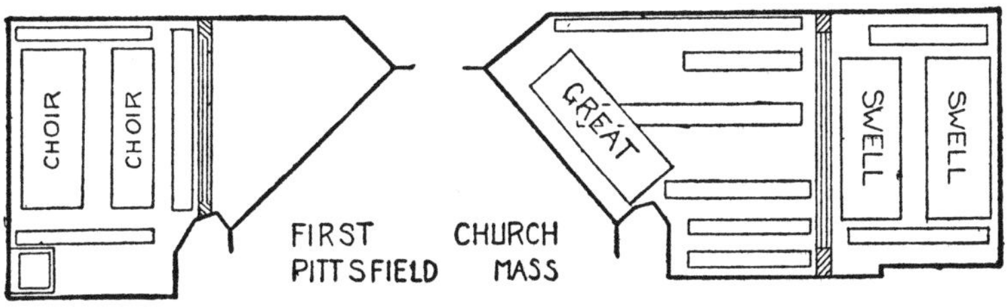

A chamber of this description was met with in the Congregational Church at Pittsfield, Mass. The chambers were very deep and narrow. By sloping the ceilings, surfacing the walls and ceilings with Keen's cement, and laying out the instrument so as to utilize the reflecting surfaces to the best

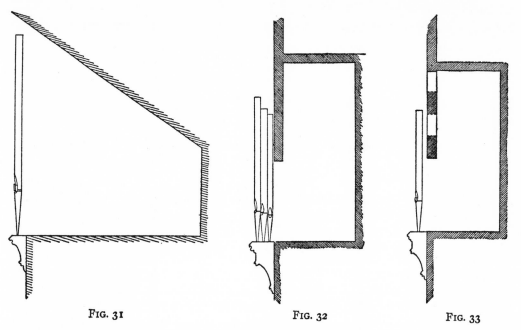

FIG. 31   FIG. 32   FIG. 33

advantage, a very fine result was obtained which gave no indication that the situation was not a perfect one in the beginning. (See Fig. 30.)

A further necessary step is the proper planning or laying out of the organ.

If the organ chambers are very deep and narrow, which is the worst possible formation, the ceilings should be sloped, as in Fig. 31 and the

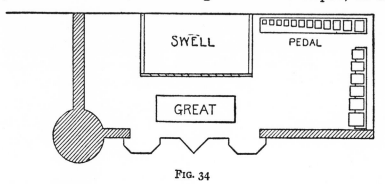

FIG. 34

entire wall and ceiling surface be covered with Keen's cement or similar hard smooth material.

An organ chamber, however ample or well proportioned, will lose much of its advantages if the opening between it and the audience room is restricted or poorly located. A chamber twenty feet high and twenty wide should have an opening of similar dimensions. If the opening is limited (as commonly happens, see Fig. 32) the resulting "pocket" is of serious disadvantage, as it prevents a certain amount of tone from issuing

and reflects it back into the chamber.   Perforating the obstruction, as at
Fig. 33 effects a cure.

If the opening extends to the full height of the chamber, but is restricted
by a side projection as at Fig. 34, the effect *may* also be poor, as the side
pocket absorbs much of the tone of the manual pipes and is also unfavorable
for the pedal pipes, as they require a position affording the utmost freedom
for their speech, and outlet for the tone.   It will be seen by a reference to
Fig. 34 that the outlet from the pedal pipes to the arch opening is greatly
restricted between the side of the arch opening and the swell-box.   This
condition is unfavorable in two ways, *i. e.*, it smothers the pedal organ and
wastes a considerable
proportion of the
manual tone.

Fig. 35 shows the
same organ chamber
seen in Fig. 34.   The
plan of the organ,
however, is entirely
different.   The
"pocket" is now used

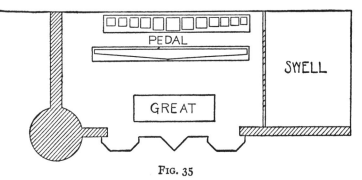

FIG. 35

as a swell-box and its walls are utilized as reflecting surfaces, as they are
covered with Keen's cement.   The pedal organ is now exactly opposite
the arch opening and no portion of the tone is obstructed or absorbed.

Figs. 34 and 35 offer a very good example of the manner in which an
instrument may be made effective, or indifferently so, by the way in which
it is planned.   In this particular case, the result depends on the organ builder
as the architect has made adequate provision for the organ.

The higher the organ chamber is above the main floor of the edifice, the
flatter the ceiling may be.   But if an organ-room were fourteen feet wide and
twenty feet deep and its floor were twelve feet above the main floor, its ceiling
should be at an angle of at least forty degrees and if there were but a single
chamber of this character, it would prohibit two expression boxes which any
well ordered three-manual instrument should have, as expression boxes cannot be placed one behind the other.

These cases more commonly arise in buildings having a proscenium, as
an auditorium or theater; an organ chamber having this formation is not
favorable and should be avoided if possible.

In some cases a basement offers the only opportunity for an installation.
This plan may be developed successfully if provision is made for properly
conveying the tone from the organ to the audience room.

In Trinity Cathedral, Cleveland, Ohio, an extension Tuba is placed in the
basement at the end of the nave in a chamber constructed as in Fig. 36,

which shows a cross section of a rectangular chamber directly below the auditorium floor. This chamber is lined with the usual Keen's cement. The tone passes through the swell-shades B and is directed upward by a solid concrete reflector, where it enters the auditorium through a cast copper grille.

Dust falling through the grille and landing on the reflector falls through the trap A into the space below.

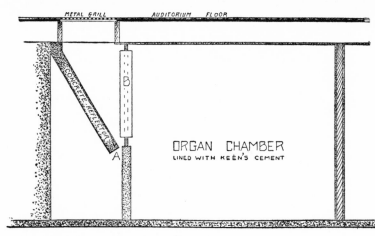

FIG. 36

This is a remarkably successful installation. A similar plan may be followed with residence organs where opportunity is lacking above stairs.

Fig. 37 shows two organ chambers of equal dimensions, one of which is good and the other poor. The one at the right is so narrow that its side walls are of no value as sound reflectors and the rear wall will be entirely covered by pedal pipes by a poor builder or by a swell-box by a good builder, so it will be of less value as a sound reflector than the side walls. In an organ chamber as narrow as this, the sound from the pipes may be projected towards the open side but at an angle too slight to be of material value.

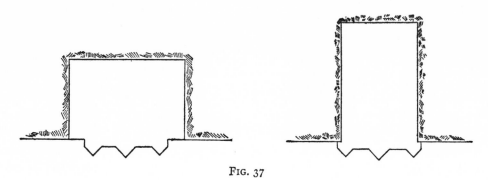

FIG. 37

In the other example, the greater width of the chamber would permit of a sound carried at this same angle to issue from the organ, and its shallow formation brings the entire instrument further forward, and as much of the rear wall is uncovered it reflects the tone directly forward.

If two instruments voiced exactly alike were placed in the same room in

FIG. 38

two chambers of the proportions shown in Fig. 37 so that a comparison could be made, a difference in effectiveness of at least 50% would be found in favor of the wide shallow space. The higher these chambers are the more alike they become, but the wider space will always be the superior one.

FRONT PIPES

In most organs there are a number of pipes that are available for display or show pipes. The lower notes of the metal stops of 16′ or 8′ pitch are suitable for this purpose. If the organ is a small one, the Great Open Diapason will be the only stop from which such pipes may be taken. In larger instruments the Great 16′ and 8′ Diapason Basses, the pedal 32′ or 16′ Violone, and possibly a few of the lower notes of a Great Dulciana, Gamba, or Erzähler are suitable for this purpose.

If an organ has fifty pipes which in point of size and locality permit of their use as show pipes, and the architects' design calls for seventy-five pipes, it is obvious that the additional twenty-five pipes must be dummies, so-called. Some architects are averse to the use of dummies and insist that all show pipes shall speak and so make difficulty for the organ builder who finds it inconvenient to incorporate extraneous material into an already complete instrument.

The architects' design usually demands pipes of equal length on opposite sides of a screen. If the pipes are "speakers" no two will be of the same speaking length as they are cut out at the back in order to give the proper pitch. Any addition in excess of the speaking length of a pipe must therefore be "dummy."

The only way to avoid the use of dummies is to show each pipe at its true length regardless of symmetry and to limit the show pipes to a number that can be taken from the basses of the specification as it stands, the balance of the space to be filled out with woodwork, grilles, panels, etc.

A number of the old world cases show the pipes at their true length. They also show a profuse use of dummy pipes, as in the cut Fig. 38, where groups of inverted pipes may be seen with others resting on their toes, a most illogical arrangement from the ultra idealistic point of view, but very satisfactory to look at and affording at the same time an ancient precedent for the use of dummy pipes.

An organ screen in which no dummy pipes are used will more likely suffer in their avoidance than in their use. The organ screen should harmonize with its visible surroundings and not with its invisible interior which concerns the ear and not the eye.

An organ case may contain wood carvings of birds, angels, cherubs, gargoyles, prophets, near prophets, vines, grapes, foliage, or any conceivable object in creation; all dummies, and none of which are actually necessary.

A silent pipe is no more a dummy than the bunch of quartered-oak grapes on the woodwork which supports it.

It would seem that the occasional architect has selected for exclusion from the organ screen the one thing that is inherently necessary and has the justification of ancient precedent.

Front pipes should be spaced as widely apart as a good appearance will permit; otherwise the tone cannot issue between them. This is especially necessary where the show pipes reach the ceiling of the organ chamber, as in this event the tone can issue only between the show pipes.

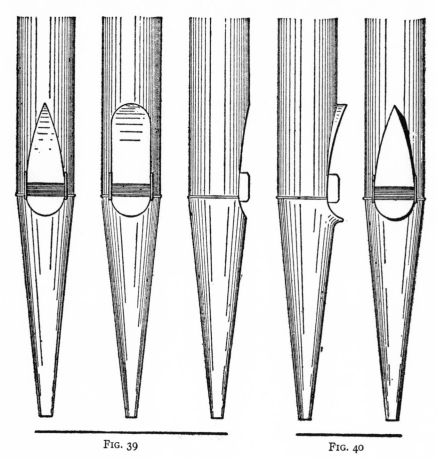

FIG. 39   FIG. 40

Grill work or perforated panels offer less obstruction to the tone of an organ than front pipes, as the percentage of opening to solid is much larger. It is also obvious that if front pipes are made as small in diameter as is consistent with a good appearance, a larger number will be required to fill a given area and a correspondingly greater number of openings between the pipes will be provided.

The accompanying drawings show various ways of constructing the mouths of display pipes, the simpler and less expensive forms being shown at

Fig. 39. Fig. 40 shows a more elaborate and handsomer construction having a raised bay leaf which may be either pointed or arched.

The accompanying table gives the diameters and lengths of bodies of pipes that are available for display purposes, and which are named in the first paragraph of this chapter. The lengths of the tapered feet are not given as they may be varied within a reasonable limit.

If the panel work of the organ case is sufficiently high, it will interfere with a proper circulation and cause an out-of-tune condition in cold weather, due to a pocketing of cold air in the lower portion of the instrument. Openings should be made as near the floor as possible, to permit a free circulation. Registers may be provided for this purpose or the panels "1," Fig. 41, in the organ case may be slightly set back from their supports "2" as shown, by the introduction of short dowels "3." This expedient is also favorable for the tone of any portion of the instrument which may otherwise be obstructed by the case work.

Radiators or steam pipes should not be placed within the organ chamber as the heat from either is liable to cause excessive dryness and

		C	#	D	#	E	F	#	G	#	A	#	B
32 Ft. Ped. Violone 36 Pipes	Diameter	9½	9	8½	8	7⅝	7⅜	7⅛	6⅞	6½	6¼	6	5¾
	Speaking Length	34-6	32-5	30-8	28-11	27-2	25-9	24-4	23-0½	20-6	19-4	18-2	17-3
16 Ft. Ped. Violone 24 Pipes	Diameter	5½	5⅛	5	4¾	4½	4⅜	4⅛	4	3⅞	3⅝	3½	3⅜
	Speaking Length	16-3	15-3½	14-5	13-7	12-10½	12-2	11-6¼	10-10½	10-3	9-8	9-1	8-6½
16 Ft. Gr. Diapason 24 Pipes	Diameter	9½	9	8½	8	7⅝	7⅜	7⅛	6⅞	6½	6¼	6	5¾
	Speaking Length	16-3	15-4	14-5	13-7	12-9	12-1	11-5	10-10	10-2½	9-7½	9-1	8-7
8 Ft. First Diap. 12 or 17 Pipes	Diameter	6½	6¼	6	5¾	5½	5¼	5	4¾	4⅝	4⅛	4	3⅞
	Speaking Length	8-1½	7-8	7-2¾	6-9½	6-4¼	6-0½	5-8½	5-5¼	5-1¼	4-9¼	4-6½	4-3½
8 Ft. Second Diap. 17 Pipes	Diameter	6	5¾	5½	5⅛	5	4¾	4½	4⅜	4⅛	4	3⅞	3⅝
	Speaking Length	8-1½	7-8	7-2¾	6-9½	6-4¼	6-0½	5-8½	5-5¼	5-1¼	4-9¼	4-6½	4-3½
8 Ft. Erzahler 10 Pipes	Diameter	4½	4⅜	4 5/16	4¼	4⅛	4	3⅞	3¾	3⅝	3½		
	Speaking Length	8-7¼	8-1	7-7¼	7-1¾	6-9	6-4¼	6-0	5-7¼	5-3⅞	5-0¼		
8 Ft. Gemshorn 10 Pipes	Diameter	5	4¾	4½	4⅜	4⅛	4	3⅞	3⅝	3½	3⅜		
	Speaking Length	8-2⅜	7-9	7-4	6-11½	6-6¾	6-2¼	5-10¾	5-7¼	5-3½	5-0		
8 Ft. Dulciana 6 Pipes	Diameter	3½	3⅜	3⅛	3 1/16	2 15/16	2⅛						
	Speaking Length	8-3¾	7-10	7-4¾	6-11½	6-6¾	6-2¼						
8 Ft. Gamba 6 Pipes	Diameter	4½	4⅜	4⅛	4	3⅞	3⅝						
	Speaking Length	8-2⅜	7-9	7-4	6-11	6-6	6-1¾						

		C	#	D	#	E	F	#	G	#	A	#	B
32 Ft. Ped. Violone 36 Pipes	Diameter	5½	5⅛	5	4¾	4½	4⅜	4⅛	4	3⅞	3⅝	3½	3⅜
	Speaking Length	16-3	15-3½	14-5	13-7	12-10½	12-2	11-6¼	10-10½	10-3	9-8	9-1	8-6½
16 Ft. Ped. Violone 24 Pipes	Diameter	3⅛	3 1/16	2 15/16	2⅞	2¾	2⅝	2½	2⅜	2¼	2⅛	2	1 15/16
	Speaking Length	8-1¼	7-8	7-2¾	6-9¼	6-5½	6-1	5-9¼	5-5¼	5-1½	4-10	4-6½	4-3½
16 Ft. Gr. Diapason 24 Pipes	Diameter	5½	5⅛	5	4¾	4½	4⅜	4⅛	4	3⅞	3⅝	3½	3⅜
	Speaking Length	8-1½	7-8	7-2¾	6-9½	6-4¼	6-0½	5-8½	5-5¼	5-1¼	4-9¼	4-6½	4-3½
8 Ft. First Diap. 12 or 17 Pipes	Diameter	3 9/16	3 7/16	3⅜	3⅛	3 1/16							
	Speaking Length	4-0½	3-9½	3-7	3-4⅞	3-2½							
8 Ft. Second Diap. 17 Pipes	Diameter	3½	3⅜	3⅛	3 1/16	2 15/16							
	Speaking Length	4-0½	3-9½	3-7	3-4⅞	3-2½							

		C	#	D	#	E	F	#	G	#	A	#	B
32 Ft. Ped. Violone 36 Pipes	Diameter	3⅛	3 1/16	2 15/16	2⅞	2¾	2⅝	2½	2⅜	2¼	2⅛	2	1 15/16
	Speaking Length	8-1¼	7-8	7-2¾	6-9¼	6-5½	6-1	5-9¼	5-5¼	5-1½	4-10	4-6½	4-3

Speaking Lengths Do Not Include Feet

shrinkage in the neighboring woodwork of the organ and a consequent deterioration in the glue, which may develop serious irregularities.

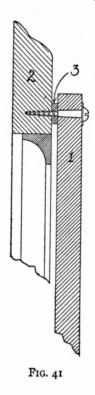

FIG. 41

BLOWING MECHANISM

The machinery for blowing the organ should not be put in the coal cellar or next to the ash pit in the furnace room. Coal dust and ashes do not improve the quality of the reeds or contribute to the good behavior of the mechanism. A perfectly dry clean space is necessary and should be provided. It may be located in a basement but should be enclosed by solidly built wooden walls. If dry air cannot be taken from the basement, a conductor should be provided to supply the air from a room above.

It is not well to run pipes carrying cold water through the blower room as condensation is liable to result and cause difficulty. A suitably dry blower room is always possible if proper ventilation is provided. A wooden enclosure of studding and matched sheathing on both sides is better than a brick one, as it is less resonant and not subject to condensation as is a brick wall where there is a lower temperature on one side of it than on the other.

The blower enclosure serves a double purpose, i. e., it keeps dust and coal ashes out of the organ and prevents the noise of the blower from being heard elsewhere, if other necessary steps are observed.

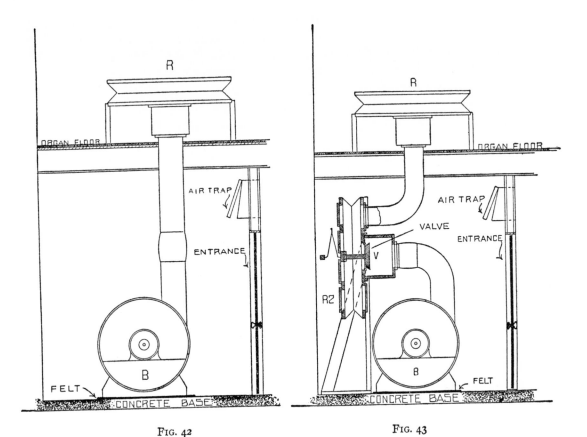

FIG. 42   FIG. 43

To insure quietness it is not sufficient to enclose the blowing mechanism as the noise of the fans will travel through the air conductor to the organ about as freely as the air itself. It is absolutely necessary to place a reservoir next the blower within the blower room and to pass the air through an automatic gate which closes as the reservoir fills. This prohibits the noise of the fan from entering the pipe which leads from the reservoir to the organ. The writer has noted the fact that this basement reservoir is omitted in a majority of cases partly on account of its extra cost and partly through lack of knowledge as to the advantage of its use.

A noisy blowing mechanism contributes to no purpose for which an auditorium is used and should not be tolerated, or regarded as a necessary evil.

Figure 42 shows an incorrect installation in which the fan communicates directly with the organ and Figure 43 shows the effect of the reservoir and its valve. When the reservoir is filled the gate is closed and therefore prevents the noise of the fan from entering the trunk which conveys the wind to the organ.

THE CONSOLE

The most desirable location for the console is that which gives most complete control of the choir and is least noticeable from the audience.

The console shown in Figure 24 is placed in an ideal position. The organist has every possible opportunity for directing the singers, for balancing organ and voices, and for hearing both as they are heard by the audience.

Positions as favorable as this, however, are somewhat uncommon. They are usually found where the organ is in a central position at either end of a building. Where the organ is divided, as it is in most Episcopal churches, it is necessary to place the console on one side of the chancel. A position opposite the front row of singers is objectionable on account of the fact that it makes the console and organist too conspicuous. A slightly elevated position in the rear of the back row of singers is satisfactory if the console is placed so that the organist faces towards the congregation. He will then be hidden from view by the console and perfectly visible to the singers. The console is so placed at St. Thomas' Church, New York City, and has proved most satisfactory.

Occasionally, choir and organist have been placed at one end of a church and the organ at the other. If, in this event, the player tries to make the remote organ balance with the singers close at hand, people near the organ will hear all organ and no voices. If, on the other hand, the organ is balanced with the voices as far as the audience is concerned, the organist and singers would find it barely audible. This position is difficult.

The console should always be located so that the organ and choir can be heard equally well by the organist, otherwise he will find it difficult to maintain a proper balance between them.

CONVENIENT CONSOLE DIMENSIONS

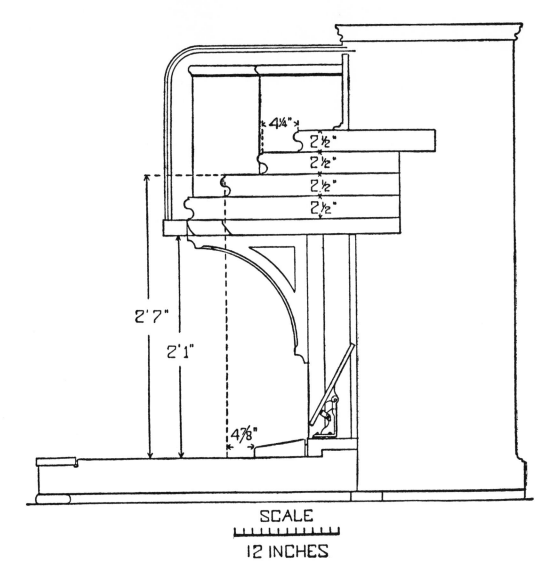

SCALE

12 INCHES

The above drawing is to scale. The perpendicular measurements are taken from the top of the center natural of the pedal keyboard. The width of a console will vary with the size of the instrument. The distances relating to the key frames remain as shown without regard to the size of the instrument.

Keyboards should be 2½" above or below each other. A distance of 4" from the front edges of one manual to a perpendicular line touching the front edges of the next above or below is usual. 4¼" is better as the fingers are less likely to interfere with a neighboring manual when staccato chords are struck.

It is important that the pedal keys should be placed sufficiently forward under the manuals, otherwise the organist has a tendency to pitch forward and his pedaling must be done in an unnatural position.

Toe pistons or combination pedals should never overhang the pedal keys as their projection prohibits freedom of movement. The swell pedals should not be set within openings cut in the toe panels as this position makes them inconvenient of access. If the toe panel is set back from the pedal sharps as shown in the drawing, suitable arrangement will be made thereby for locating combination movements above the ledge or shelf created by recessing the panel.

This plan also gives the swell pedals an open position as shown above.

The convenience of the organist should be made the first consideration of the organ builder, regardless of fads, hobbies, or economics.

THE END

Ernest M. Skinner

A Biographical Sketch

By T. SCOTT BUHRMAN

Reprinted from The American Organist, New York
Copyright 1925 Organ Interests Inc.

Ernest M. Skinner: Organ Builder

The Story of the Making of a Great Organ Builder, set forth
in a Manner Worthy of His Contributions to the Organ
Player's Art—the First of a Series of Biographies
of American Organ Builders

By T. SCOTT BUHRMAN

JOHN ALDEN used a hammer and a saw, added muscle as the motive power and intelligence as the guiding, and helped make the repairs on the May-flower that enabled that delightful ship, sailing from Plymouth on the 6th of September in 1620, to reach America some time later; and there are those who say that John Alden was the first to step ashore. It may have been unfortunate for Standish to trust Alden too far when Priscilla Mullins was to say Yes to somebody. She said it to John and not to Miles. In the ninth generation of Alden-Mullins progeny came Alice F. Skinner and her husband W. M. Skinner. And in the tenth, Ernest M. Skinner. Ernest M. Skinner also knows how to use a hammer and a saw, and has been unafraid to sail uncharted seas.

Mr. Ernest M. Skinner was born in Clarion, Penna., Jan. 15th in 1866. The M stands for—"but don't use it; I don't like it,"—which is the reason it still stands here incomplete, though a very worthy name it is. Taunton, Mass., gave his father a position as chorister in the Unitarian Church and himself his first contact with music. His father organized an opera company in Taunton and gave the Gilbert and Sullivan operas, taking his ten-year-old son to rehearsals and performances, and creating in him a "great love for the music of these operas." This great love went a bit farther and included the prima donna, without serious consequences nor the formation of the habit. This second love ultimately passed, and a love for the organ took its place. The father has gone, but the mother still lives (in Pasadena, Calif.) to enjoy the ad-

miration the music world is glad to give her son and his handiwork. Another group of admirers intimately concerned with the position of Mr. Skinner in the world of organ building is composed of his wife, née Mabel Hastings to whom he was married in 1893, their three children, and their children's three grand-children.

The organ grew in interest and Mr. Edward M. French, organist of the Taunton Baptist Church, is he who had the privilege of giving Mr. Ernest M. Skinner his first official contact with the instrument he was ultimately to create as his own product; Mr. French engaged E. M. as his blow-boy, and being a kindly gentleman with a big heart, went a little further and permitted him to inspect the marvelous interior of the Baptist organ. His blow-boy's first discovery in the arts of organ-building came when he found and cured the cause of a leak in the bellows. Forty-six years ago this blow-boy plied his honorable trade while workmen made repairs on an organ—and his curiosity and admiration drew him on, and on, and on.

More incentive than satisfaction resulted from all these experiences and ultimately the young man decided to build an organ of his own, with a drum-and-pins to play it, like the Swiss music box. It remained merely a decision; the drums-and-pin idea was translated some forty years later in an automatic player that makes an artist live forever in the perforations of a paper roll that is one of twentieth century man's achievements.

The first six months in high school went well enough, but perhaps none too jubilantly. The candy store appealed to him so thoroughly that after his first day's employment there he managed to eat enough—and has needed no candy since.

MR. ERNEST M. SKINNER

Especially posed by Mr. Skinner for readers of THE AMERICAN ORGANIST—Mr. Skinner operating the semi-automatic player invented by himself and drawing by hand his personally selected registration on the organ built by his genius and voiced under his personal supervision—proud achievements of a life-time of effort

His father considered Mr. George H. Ryder's shop a better place for the young man, and thus the organ building industry claimed its man in the city of Reading, Mass., and the broom became his first operated machine, which I contrived, at about twice the ordinary speed. I was interested in the voicing which was remote, from any possible contact with me but later a part of my duties was to act as

MR. ERNEST M. SKINNER

Studio portrait of a 10th generation descendant of John Alden, whose first contact with the organ was through the handle of the blower, whose first implement in an organ factory was a broom —and whose most recent contract · was signed with the Washington Cathedral

implement in the world of building organs. with the broom, an uninteresting thing to a man, Mr. Skinner hastened through the opening tasks of each day's work, and passed on to more interesting things. Thus the year 1886 was a great one in Skinner history. The subject speaks of it interestingly:

"My first duty was to sweep the shop after which I wound trackers. After a little while I wound them with a hand a helper to Wm. H. Dolbier, Mr. Ryder's voicer and tuner. I desired to know the theory of setting a temperament but found it was a secret. 'Charlie' Moore, a reed voicer for Samuel Pierce, finally told me to sharp the fourths and flatten the fifths and this is all the instruction I ever had in the art of tuning. I bought a piano hammer and practised on my father's piano by putting it out of tune. I remember my joy the first time I succeeded in killing the 'wolf.' As time went on and my small experience found opportunity I hunted tuning methods and possibilities to a finish.''

In later years Mr. Skinner was destined to spend many months in tuning

ple, easy method. Perhaps it lends itself to an un-orchestral stiffness? Perhaps orchestral richness of ensemble comes much better through the fourth and fifth tuning throughout? At least all Skinner Organ tuners must use the fourth and

THEY UNKNOWINGLY BUILT AN ORGAN-BUILDER

Mr. Edward M. French at the console of his organ in the Baptist Church of Taunton, Mass., especially posed for readers of THE AMERICAN ORGANIST. Mr. French is still playing the identical organ that Mr. Skinner "blew"—his first actual contact with the world of the organ, the very same organ our illustration presents

exclusively, and he developed a practise of setting the temperament on every class of register, including mixtures, by ignoring the octave and using fourths and fifths alone; he developed it into a speedy process and one that could be done accurately in spite of its apparent difficulties: many other tuners have been personally instructed in this new method of voicing by Mr. Skinner himself. He gave his broom to other incipient organ builders. Greater implements called loudly for his hand and heart.

The method of tuning has an important bearing on the finished product that bears Mr. Skinner's name. Common practise dictated that the middle octave of the 4′ Principal should be chosen for the battle ground in setting the temperament; and that was done by fourths and fifths. All the rest of the Principal was then tuned by octaves, and the rest of the organ by unisons and octaves. A sim-

fifth method and discard the octave and unison.

Mr. Skinner's contention is that there is so much difference between the timbre of a Diapason and a Tuba or a Flute or a Vox Humana that it is unsatisfactory to attempt to tune them by unisons against each other, and that the independent tuning of each register by fourths and fifths on itself, with occasional testings by unisons and octaves on itself and on the fundamental 4′ Principal, is one of the things that have helped him win the admiration of so many organists who are Skinner advocates. There's an idea for anybody who wants it. Another idea is worth recording: Mr. Skinner prefers the two-octave or three-octave interval to the unison or octave, for the reason that the beats are easier to detect, for obvious reasons.

Now to return to the evolution of a great builder. We are still in the day of hand work, the day when machinery in organ building was unknown, the day when Mr. Skinner's eight-hours were applied direct to woods and metals without the intervention of machines. The Mutin factory in Paris is still that way. England has gone far in the creation of machinery to build organ parts, and Ameri-

An incidental outside job took him to the residence of Mr. Montgomery Sears, whose organ he tuned and regulated so satisfyingly that his patron decided to send him to Europe for study and observation. About the first thing Mr. Skinner did when he landed in England was to learn that the Maine had been blown up,

THE FIRST SKINNER FACTORY

Which Mr. Skinner acquired when he became an independent organ builder. From this little building came the organs that carried the first Skinner Organ name-plates. The building seemed to grow smaller as the man grew bigger; the latter soon outgrew the former. Photo especially posed by Mr. Skinner for readers of THE AMERICAN ORGANIST—another example of the courtesy Mr. Skinner has always shown the organ profession

ca has gone a decade beyond England.

After four years in his first position Mr. Skinner "was fired one morning by a new Irish foreman," and he promptly took employment with Mr. George S. Hutchings of Boston, working in the Hutchings factory as tuner, then going to Mr. Jesse Woodberry, also of Boston, who promised him employment as traveling erector—the idea of ripping the thing apart to see how all of it was made, had much too great an appeal for the growing organ builder. But the Woodberry promise was not made good and the Hutchings factory again employed him as voicer— which the fates kindly changed to the position as draftsman, in which capacity he remained for twelve years. The new Hutchings tubular and electric actions owed their origin and development to Mr. Skinner's ingenuity.

and the second was to enquire where St. George's Hall happened to be located at the moment.

"I asked a newsboy. He pointed it out and said, 'I'm going there Saturday night.' I went Saturday night—admission two cents. Dr. Peace played operatic airs on a big Vox Humana to a crowd that filled the hall. After each number there was clapping and yelling and a spontaneous expression of enthusiasm in full keeping with what we hear in these United States at a ball game. There was no doubt whatever that Dr. Peace played to that crowd just what would please them most and that they thoroughly enjoyed it. I then and there acquired an overwhelming sympathy with the idea of music for the common public as well as for the musician."

The St. George's Hall visit was happily

fortuitous, for he met Mr. Henry Willis, Jr. What this led to is best told in Mr. Skinner's words:

"At St. George's Hall I was very fortunate in meeting Henry Willis, Jr., who was most agreeable to me. He sent a man with me to look at one of his organs and

land too he found the action impossible, and the tone bad. of an incident in Belgium we shall let Mr. Skinner tell in his own way:

"Leaving the train at Antwerp to hear the celebrated chimes, I asked directions of various pedestrians but nobody under-

"WITH CARPENTERS AND WOOD-BUTCHERS"

He built the organ for the College of the City of New York, the first organ to come from this new Skinner factory, when his hundred men with the exception of one went on strike—which proves that Mr. Skinner can build a whole organ from nails to tone. The studio and music-roll building occupies the here vacant lot in the foreground. Many organists think the sun rises and sets over this particular group of buildings three hundred sixty-five times each year

permitted me to take measurements of reeds and a tremolo which was fine in effect and noiseless. Afterwards at the dinner table he showed me where I had overlooked much of importance and further instructed me in the fundamental principles of reed voicing which were unknown in America as far as my experience goes.

"I had read of the Willis Tuba on 22" wind in St. George's Hall. When I heard it I was wild with enthusiasm. It was so incredibly fine and superior to anything I had ever heard. I owe everything I know of the trumpet family to Henry Willis, Senior and Junior. I was given the freedom of the St. George's Hall organ and I made the most of it."

Though Mr. Skinner was greatly impressed and benefitted by the Willis reeds, he was not favorably impressed with the action of current British organs, finding it clumsy and antiquated. In Hol-

stood English. I knew then how the poor dago feels in this country who 'no spik Englis.' By and by I heard a man say, 'I played hell with'em,' and it sounded like a benediction. He directed me to the chimes."

Of his meeting with Widor and Vierne, Mr. Skinner shall also tell:

"In Paris I met Widor and Vierne. I had an interpreter, a German who spoke Francaise and English too. I had a letter to Widor given by Mr. Sears. He took me to 'San' Sulpice. There was a service on. Vierne, assistant to Widor, was extemporizing upon a Gregorian theme after it was sung by the choir at the other end of the church. I have never heard anything so lofty in conception before or since. The French organ is wonderful in the French church, always having every acoustical advantage that location can give."

Of French organ-building Mr. Skinner

could not hold a high opinion; the action, console, etc. seemed anything but progressive to the American builder's eyes—and today they are no better than they were then. The Cavaille-Coll factory seems to

MR. ARTHUR HUDSON MARKS

President of the Skinner Organ Company, an organ fan of the self-starter, perpetual-motion type. Mr. Marks' foresight and courage made possible many of the later achievements of the Company he heads

have adopted the past as its model and continues to ignore the present and the future. Magnificent cathedrals give magnificent tone—and when they fail to give it, the imagination of the visitor most frequently supplies it.

Upon returning to America Mr. Skinner resumed his work in the Hutchings factory, and there remained till 1901. Of the history of that period Mr. Skinner says:

"About the year 1901 to my great regret and through no act of Mr. Hutchings or myself, I left my old friend and partner and hung my shingle out on a shack in South Boston. I started with $4,300.00 capital, part of which came from royalties on a piano accenting device now known as the themodist upon which I

took out a patent in 1900 or thereabout. It was hard sledding. When I look back upon those early years I fail to see how I contrived to build so many large organs on so limited a capital. During this period I built the organs in the Evangelical Lutheran Church, Central Park West and Sixty-Sixth Street, New York City; Grace Church, Plymouth Church, Brooklyn, and others of similar character."

The themodist of which Mr. Skinner speaks is a device applied to mechanical piano players which accents certain notes and makes it possible to bring the melody forward by mechanical means about as well as it can be done by the human player. What a different story might be told had Mr. Skinner invented his themodist after instead of before his association with Mr. Arthur Hudson Marks, patron of the organ building arts and financier of the Skinner factory.

Life is not all sweetness and joy; there is a little of everything in it. Mr. Skinner once said that it would be safer for a man to go out into the streets and pick the first few men he should see, for his business partners, rather than to do as he did when he selected from among his friends two men to be associated with him in the Hutchings factory. These two friends schemed him out entirely—a friendly little trick humanity still plays now and then. On the way out, however, Mr. Skinner incidentally stopped at a place that is known as the Skinner Organ Factory. Where is the Hutchings factory now? Life plays strange tricks. Mr. Horace Marden became a friend of Mr. Skinner when the latter was taken into the Ryder factory, and when the former went to the Hutchings factory he remembered his friend and took him in. John Brennan went to the Ryder factory in the place of Mr. Marden and goes down in history as having been blind enough to discharge the only man who can save him from oblivion in the history of organ building.

A stock company was formed in 1905 with subscriptions from Mr. George Foster Peabody of New York and from business friends in Worcester, Mass. The new organization was the background out of which grew the organs of City College,

St. John Divine, St. Thomas, Columbia, all of New York City, and Trinity Cathedral of Cleveland. The firm built about two hundred instruments in all. The office force at this time consisted of Mr. Ernest M. Skinner, one bookkeeper, one stenographer, and one draftsman.

And then one day he became acquainted with Mr. Arthur Hudson Marks—and the Skinner Organ Company of 677 Fifth Avenue, New York, N. Y., is operated from the finest commercial organ studio in the world. It required the business mind to conceive an appropriate headquarters for the arts of organ building. The Studio has not been an expense; it has paid for itself many times over.

The first Skinner Organ in the world was a two-manual instrument of seven stops, three of them interchangeable, for the Unitarian Church of Ludlow, Vermont. Interchangeable is Mr. Skinner's term for borrowing or duplexing or whatever one may call it. In his own schemes he uses it only to avoid duplication in limited specifications or for an occasional special effect. The largest instrument built by the Skinner Organ Company is that for the Cleveland Auditorium, an organ of five manuals and one hundred sixty stops, only two of which were extensions, and no interchangeables or borrows.

The drawing of a specification is rather a conscientious business with Mr. Skinner. He is perfectly willing to draw specifications for organs to be composed of pipe-work built and voiced by the Skinner factory, but he considers that he does not know enough about the complicated subjects involved to write specifications covering the pipes built and voiced in other factories. In other words the writing of names of stops into a supposedly satisfying organ ensemble is a matter that one of the men who know most about it is least willing to lightly undertake. Yet we roundly condemn a builder and a factory when they, compelled by current practises in the organ world to accept "specifications" drawn by incompetent organists, turn out a product that is unsatisfactory, unscientific, and inartistic.

Most of the Skinner products are joint-ly designed by the purchaser's organist and Mr. Skinner or Mr. William E. Zeuch of the Skinner Company. There are about five hundred Skinner Organs in the world today, with perhaps fifty more under contract. California contributed $350,000. in contracts in less than two years. In New York City there are nine Skinner 32' Diapasons.

Eighty registers will make a representative Skinner Organ and give the purchaser a sample of about every tone color Mr. Skinner uses. Every pipe in a Skinner Organ is a Skinner-made pipe, including reeds and Harp, though the Chimes are but rarely Skinner-made.

Has Mr. Skinner any favorite organ tones? I believe he has. I tried to discover them. So far as I got, I learned that his favorites were all those lying alphabetically between Aeoline and Vox Humana, with a tolerable preference also for those down to Zartflote. If we never can see Mr. Skinner seated at the console of the organ in Skinner Studio, hear him fondle the tones, watch him operate the player when at semi-automatic operation, all of which I have done, we never shall understand him. A prima donna must be a delightful thing to fall in love with. I hope he has not tried it since his boyhood days. I know he has fallen in love with something different, and that affection is an intense devotion, though not an enslavement. He is no wild-eyed artist with all feeling and no sense. He is very much a normal business man, sometimes a t.b.m. very much alive. He has merely mastered the organ; the organ hasn't by any means mastered him. Doubt if anything will ever fully master him.

Mr. Skinner's invention and development of the automatic player for Skinner Organs is surprising. When fully automatic it will do everything, not forgetting to first cancel every stop and coupler on the entire organ so that it may paint its own tonal pictures. By a special device its registrational control of every stop of the full organ is unlimited, and more masterful than ever a human player can be. Interpretively it is marvelous; it will reproduce accents, crescendos, ritards, pauses, just as faithfully as the sun rises.

My special visit to the Skinner Studio was pleasantly terminated by the arrival of Mr. Henry Willis, Jr., the present head of the Willis factory in England, and son of the Henry Willis, Jr., mentioned in connection with Mr. Skinner's well as in America, but Mr. Skinner is dynamic while Mr. Willis is cautious. But the dynamic and the cautious chummed together in excellent fellowship and Mr. Skinner found the long sought

WHAT THEY KNOW ABOUT ORGAN BUILDING

would fill a dozen books. Mr. Skinner has written one short but practical book on the subject, but his friend, Mr. Henry Willis, Jr., the 3d Henry Willis of organ building fame, has yet to write his. Photographed by the Author in the Skinner Studio, New York when Mr. Skinner kindly placed at the amateur photographer's disposal half of the Studio staff for the holding of lights. Mr. Skinner's book deals exclusively with a few chief items necessary to the successfully artistic modern organ

tioned in connection with Mr. Skinner's first visit to Egland. Here then I had two great builders instead of one. Hobbies were brought up and Mr. Skinner carried out a motion-picture camera with full directions how to operate.

"How fearfully serious you Americans are with your hobbies," commented Mr. Willis.

"Who makes the best organs in Great Britain today?" I asked him.

"Why, that's a queer question to ask me!" That's all I could get out of Mr. Willis. Had I asked such a question of the subject of this sketch, I know full well what answer I should have gotten and with what speed. We know that pride of craftsmanship rages in England just as

opportunity to repay the house of Willis for the many courtesies shown him on English soil.

The "profound impression" made upon Mr. Skinner by the Willis 16' low C Trombone has endured. The first Skinner replica was made in the Hutchings factory immediately upon his return and the many fine reeds in which Mr. Skinner takes such pride are partly a result. There is the Skinner French Horn, the English Horn, the Orchestral Oboe. Of another family is the Erzahler with its curious name. I enquired about the name. Mr. Skinner had the pipes on the voicing machine and was testing their tone. It struck him that his new pipes were "garrulous with a chatty sort of friendliness."

He turned to a German employee—

"Do you know any word that means talkative, garrulous?"

"Erzahler."

Erzahler was short enough to go on a stop-knob, it was euphonious; what more could he ask?

As to the ethics of selling, of competition, or cooperation, in the world of the organ, Mr. Skinner is anything but enthusiastic, nor does he see any remedy. His own psychology sees no barrier whatever to the immediate consummation of the plan of pooled patents, such as

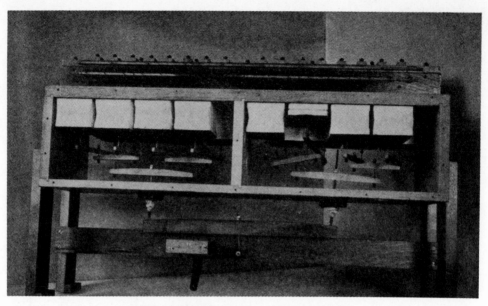

THE SKINNER CRESCENDO MOTOR

One of the great defects of the modern organ is the lack of control of the crescendo shutters when the old direct-connected tracker gives way to the modern mechanical swell-shutter control. Mr. Skinner's 16-point Crescendo Motor has been the admiration of all who have used it. Note the multiplicity of leverages, by which the player has sixteen definite stages of crescendo and diminuendo at his command. The collapse of each one of the sixteen bellows gives a small but definite motion to the shutters

The theater, thinks Mr. Skinner, is doing its music missionary work more largely through the orchestra than the organ. The theater organ is only beginning to draw the right kind of players, for the attitude of the profession has been a serious influence for ill; instead of fostering and using, we have allowed others to lower and abuse; only a few of our best men and women have had the foresight and the ability, let us not forget the latter, to attack the theater problem. Mr. Skinner's newest and best theater organ is that in the Colony on Broadway, New York, where Mr. John Priest is organist.

For the high class church organist Mr. Skinner sees a greater demand than supply, meaning not that there are too few organists for the churches, but too few five-thousand-dollar men and women. "Artistic perception of what's good and what's not," is the thing we need most.

brought speedy perfection to the automobile; in fact he sees without protest devices of his own, some patented, some not, in constant use in other factories. His Crescendo Shutter motor, for example, would be of inestimable benefit to the advancement of the art of organ building, were every builder permitted or persuaded to use it. He has invented a special method of moving the shutters open for the first few movements of the engine that eliminates the present handicap of the burst of crescendo at the start, followed by almost no crescendo for the rest of the distance.

When is an organ a failure ? When the other fellow builds it. When is a recital all that is bad and little that is good ? When the other fellow plays it. We are all more or less like that. Has Mr. Skinner built any poor organs ? Who hasn't ? I'm not nominating Mr. Ernest M. Skinner for a seat among the immortal saints of heaven. I am merely trying to put on record the aims and achievements of one

possibilities of the organ. The symphonic orchestral colors have always seemed to me to be as necessary to the organ as to

THE WORLD'S LARGEST SKINNER

in the Auditorium, Cleveland, Ohio. Photograph especially taken for readers of The American Organist, through the courtesy of Mr. Edwin Arthur Kraft, official concert organist of the Auditorium. Mr. Kraft is frequently heard at this console over the radio

of the world's very great organ builders, largely perhaps because that thing has never yet been satisfactorily done and we the players owe so much to our contemporary American builders. It is they who have made us the supreme organists of the age.

Every great achievement of man is the product not of hands but of the imagination. I want Mr. Skinner to tell how the ever-present Skinner French Horn came into being.

"What I have done in creating the Skinner Organ is due almost wholly to a love of music, plus a mediocre inventive faculty, plus an unbounded belief in the

the orchestra and so under the stimulus of some great orchestral or operatic work I have worked out all the orchestral colors and have included them in the Skinner Organs. When the organ was planned for Williams College, Mr. Salter insisted on a French Horn and so one was written into the specifications. Before that time Richard Strauss' Salome was given by the Manhattan Opera Company and I had heard eight French Horns in unison in the Salome Dance and was from that time on determined that the French Horn should be added to the voices of the organ if I could ever get the opportunity to work it out.

"The opportunity came and after much research the French Horn took its place in the Skinner Organ.

"I had a better French Horn than I really expected for the tone was not only there but the so-called bubble was also present.

"The reception of the orchestral colors by the various organists has been most curious and follows as definite a law as the law of probabilities in an insurance schedule.

"Those who are interested in music for music's sake, the orchestra, opera, piano and any good music have welcomed these voices. The Classicist, the Ritualist and the Purist have fought and disapproved them. One writer says they are neither 'fish, flesh nor fowl,' but we kept on making them and now no organ is considered complete without them."

I believe Mr. Skinner is more of a tonal genius than mechanical, yet I give here a formidable list of his inventions and mechanical ideas which threaten to swamp my belief:

PNEUMATIC CRESCENDO ENGINE—that moves the shutters in absolute synchronization with the movement of the foot;

KEY PNEUMATIC—invented thirty years ago and still standing the test of time and continued use in modern instruments;

ELECTRO-MAGNET—"and mountings which cannot be mal-adjusted and which I believe, taken together with the Key Pneumatic, is the oldest surviving electro-pneumatic action now in active manufacture;"

ELECTRO-PNEUMATIC CRESCENDO ENGINE—noiseless and "sympathetic to the most exacting desires of the organist;"

SLIDERLESS WIND CHEST—

REGISTER CRESCENDO—a mechanism directly connected to the Pedal and "made possible only through the invention of the closed circuit stop action now used the world over;"

CRESCENDO SHUTTER design—

ADJUSTABLE COMBINATION PISTON—with independent motor for each piston;

ELECTRO-PNEUMATIC COUPLER SWITCH—"consisting of a single unit, the motor and switch being one and the same;"

AUXILIARY MANUAL WIND CHESTS—for bases of 8′ and 16′ registers, in lieu of the old method of conveying wind to them through long conductors;

RESERVOIR SPRINGS—instead of weights, to maintain even pressure for all conditions;

AUTOMATIC PLAYER developments by which each wind-duct is used for a maximum of seven different operations; it will play its own note, or the octave above, or the octave below, or with either of them, and it will draw a stop, or take off all other stops; the roll width thus remains 10⅛″ (otherwise it would be 28″);

RECIPROCATING PNEUMATIC TRANSFORMERS—"by which wind entering at the top issues at the side at double the pressure; fully automatic and motionless unless wind is being used; inverting valves will change 100% + pressure to 90%—.

Mr. Skinner also claims to be the first American builder to adopt as a standard the concave-radiating pedal clavier with the thirty-two-note compass. Among the registers especially designed by Mr. Skinner or peculiarly characteristic of his work are the following, as taken from the list furnished by Mr. Skinner himself for this sketch; in each case we give the organ in which the register was first used (all are 8′ unless otherwise noted):

ERZAHLER—Christ Church, Hartford, Conn.
ORCHESTRAL OBOE—Tompkins Avenue Congregational Church, Brooklyn, N. Y.
ENGLISH HORN (8′and 16′)—City College, New York
FRENCH HORN—Williams College
KLEINE ERZAHLER—Fourth Presbyterian, Chicago
GROSS GEDECKT—Second Congregational, Holyoke, Mass.
CORNO DI BASSETTO—Williams College
TUBA MIRABILIS—St. John Cathedral, New York
FRENCH TRUMPET—St. John Cathedral, New York
ORCHESTRAL BASSOON (16′)—Skinner Studio, Boston
GAMBA CELESTE—St. John Cathedral, New York
BOMBARDE (32′)—City College, New York
VIOLONE (32′)—St. John Cathedral, New York

Among other registers of especial interest to Mr. Skinner because of what he has been able to do with them are his Diapason of heavy weight, not excessive scale, narrow mouth, and on heavy wind; Salicional and Voix Celeste; Flauto Dolce and Flute Celeste Celesta and Celesta-Sub; Heckelphone, Barytone Oboe, and Unda Maris.

Mr. Skinner gives liberal credit to the many organists, famous and otherwise, who have contributed to the Skinner Organ by their criticism, suggestion, confidence and praise. Of the new corporate existence of the Skinner Organ, Mr. Skinner humorously says, in reference to his friend and financier, Mr. Arthur Hudson Marks, that "someone else is in charge of the Department of Worries!" And he continues, "If I want to sit up until two o'clock in the morning and talk organ I have Arthur Marks to sit up and talk with me. I thought I was the worst case of organ fan ever, but it looks as though there was another fully as bad, if not worse."

I have always contended that Mr. Skinner's prestige rests in part upon his mingling with the members of the organ playing profession; so far as my observation goes, he was the first and remains the most persistent patron of the players among the builders. He personally at-

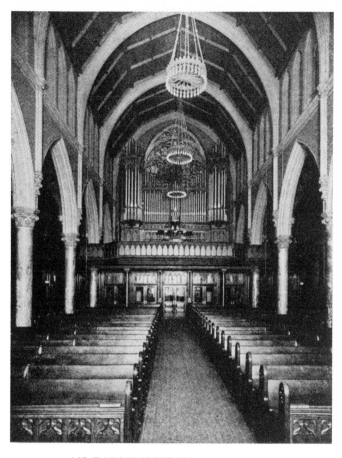

AN EARLY NEW YORK SKINNER

One of the first installations in New York City was that in Holy Trinity Lutheran where Mr. Henry F. Seibert now plays. Today Mr. Skinner fairly explodes with pride as he recounts for you his notable list of New York City Skinners. And he is as proud of the organists who play Skinner Organs as he is of the organs themselves; it's all one big Skinner Family to him

ally famous organists as organ critic for a year at a salary of five thousand dollars, just to see where and how to improve the product of the factory. Mr. Skinner doesn't have to employ a man or pay the

tends their conventions, and when they ask him to make an address at a meeting anywhere, where two or three are gathered together, he not only makes the promise but makes the speech as well. No doubt there is somewhat of a reaction that follows, and benefits the man and builder; I believe it very largely improves the product too. I believe an organ built after hearing the advice and criticism of the players, will be a better organ. A commercial genius in the organ world told me that he had advised his principal to employ one of the half-dozen nation-

salary; he gets the same thing for nothing. He has had the luck to build organs for men who did care, and most of them have cared enough to criticize as well as praise. If a man is a supreme genius he may get along well enough without criticism; a supreme genius is born once every three centuries. The rest of mankind finds perfection through the only short-cut to success that I know, namely, the short-cut of unbiased criticism of disinterested or positively antagonistic outsiders.

This sketch began with Mr. Ernest M.

Skinner, it should likewise conclude with him. It has tried in between to discern and portray the atmosphere, the essence, the spirit, of the thing Mr. Skinner typifies to so many organists. And it has tried to put on record, for the first time in history, the honest, simple true story of the making of a great artist and organ builder. If it has been successful in conveying to the reader the truth that Mr. Skinner has been successful in the building of organs because he has loved his task so thoroughly, worked with all that was his, even as you and I, and attained thereby and in no other way; if it has told of the man who began with a broom and who today finds his name marking a studio of unprecedented excellence in which is represented the quality of his works, an organ and mechanical player capable of reproducing, perpetuating an Heinrothian art—if it has done these things, it has been faithful to my every wish and has recorded in a measure somewhat fit and just a lasting tribute to a great American, a valiant warrior, a man with two eyes, both of them open lo, these many years. I like a man who has hoed a hard row of his own selection, and lived to see the harvest. He is not a financial genius; I doubt even if he is rich, save in the esteem of the organ world. It takes money to run a modern organ factory, more money than can be raised by the old methods; Mr. Skinner knows that, and he sold his troubles to Mr. Marks and the new Skinner Organ Company, retaining outside of factory control the voicing rooms under his own personal supervision. It was his voicing that made the strongest appeal to him in his youth; it is voicing that retains the appeal now.

Mr. Ernest M. Skinner is a tone-sensitive genius. To have won, and lost, and won again; to hold an ever youthful sense of humor; to keep at three score years an interest as keen as at thirty—this is the man I hope my readers may know the better and the more admire. Mr. Skinner is the first of the builders to realize the value of personal association with the players, and they have rewarded him richly—in esteem and in contracts. They have helped him create better organs, and he in turn has given them better instruments on which to practise their art. Both have profited. And this is cooperation.

ORGAN BOOKS PUBLISHED BY THE ORGAN LITERATURE FOUNDATION . . .

Mark Wicks: ORGAN BUILDING FOR AMATEURS. $15.00

H. F. Milne: THE REED ORGAN: ITS DESIGN AND CONSTRUCTION. $5.00

H. F. Milne: HOW TO BUILD A SMALL TWO-MANUAL CHAMBER
   PIPE ORGAN. $10.00

F. E. Robertson: A PRACTICAL TREATISE ON ORGAN BUILDING.
   2 Volumes. $35.00

Rev. Noel A. Bonavia-Hunt: MODERN ORGAN STOPS. $7.50

S. G. Earl: REPAIRING THE REED ORGAN AND HARMONIUM. $2.50

Reginald Whitworth: THE ELECTRIC ORGAN. $21.00

Lois Rowell: AMERICAN ORGAN MUSIC ON RECORDS. $6.00

William H. Clarke: AN OUTLINE OF THE STRUCTURE OF THE
   PIPE ORGAN. $8.00

John Ogasapian: ORGAN BUILDING IN NEW YORK CITY, 1700–1900. $20.75

Ernest M. Skinner: THE MODERN ORGAN. $12.00

FORTHCOMING TITLES . . .

Hilborne L. Roosevelt: CHURCH, CHAPEL, CONCERT AND CHAMBER ORGANS.
   (Trade Catalogue).   Available Fall, 1978

George Ashdown Audsley: DUO-ART AEOLIAN PIPE ORGAN.   Winter, 1978

New York Church Organ Co.:   VOCALIAN (REED) ORGANS.   Trade
   Catalogue.   Winter, 1978

Price subject to change without notice.

Orders under $20.00 please add 50¢ for postage and handling.

Send for our catalogue of over 800 items.

THE ORGAN LITERATURE FOUNDATION, Braintree, Mass. 02184

DATE DUE

ILL 3-5-86			
ILL - ALA 12-30-90			
ILL4622907 12-7-94			
ILL9481297 2-4-88			
JUL 1 7 2007			